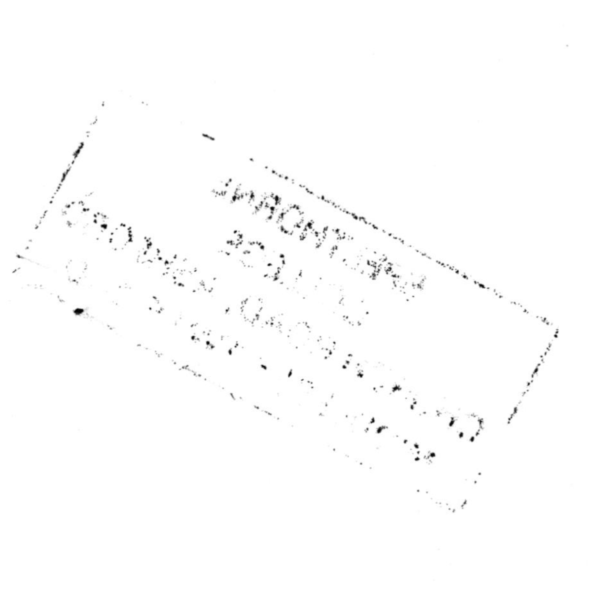

FURNITURE
& FURNISHINGS

The Diagram Group

Editor Randal Gray
Editorial assistant James Dallas
Art director Darren Bennett
Artists Peter Crossman, Brian Hewson, Lee Lawrence, Paul McCauley, Philip Patenall, Micky Pledge, Tim Scrivens

STUDIO VISTA
an imprint of
Cassell
Villiers House, 41/47 Strand
London WC2N 5JE

First published 1990

British Library Cataloguing in Publication Data
White, Antony
Furniture and furnishings: a visual guide. (Visual guides to the decorative arts.)
1. Furniture, history
I. Title II. Robertson, Bruce III. Series
749.2

ISBN 0-289-80036-6

Printed in Portugal by Resopal Indústria Gráfica, Ida. – Sintra

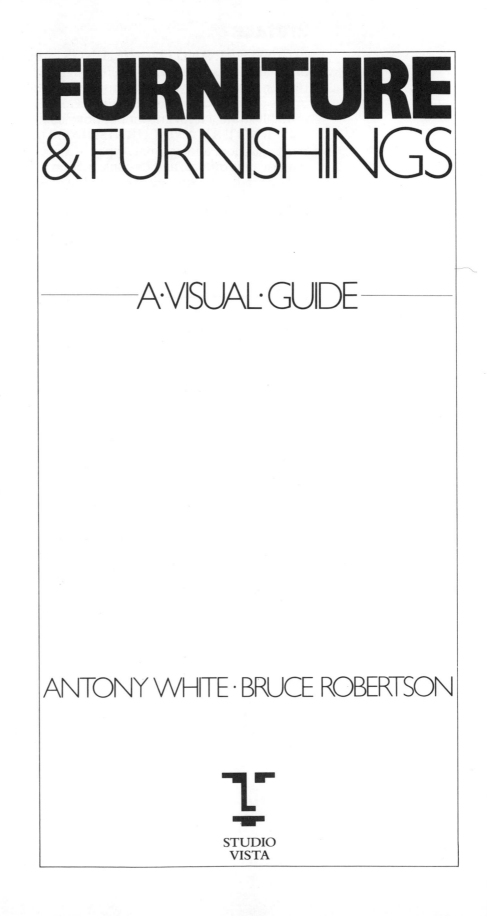

FURNITURE & FURNISHINGS

A·VISUAL·GUIDE

ANTONY WHITE · BRUCE ROBERTSON

STUDIO
VISTA

Preface

FURNITURE AND FURNISHINGS is the second of a series of visual guides which have been designed as ingenious reference books for students, enthusiasts and collectors—as books to be used both as field guides to identify objects as seen, or to illustrate a term known but not visually understood.

FURNITURE AND FURNISHINGS provides a guide to most common, and unusual, types of European and American furniture, and its construction and decoration.

The reader can start either from the glossary text or the plates, either by looking up a term or name which will then be cross referred to the illustrations, or by using the plates of illustrations to identify a term and hence its alphabetical place in the text.

The illustration plates start by providing line drawings of all the major types of beds; chairs; chests and boxes; cupboards; desk and bureaux; sofas; stands; tables and other miscellaneous objects. They provide a clear guide in alphabetical order to the naming and the function of the object.

These plates are followed by specific drawings demonstrating the construction of beds, chairs, desks and cabinets, and tables. The different types and forms of feet, legs, hinges, handles, pediments and pilasters are further illustrated; as are the principles of turnery and joinery.

A further section of plates show the principal forms of surface decoration and moulding used in the ornamentation of furniture.

The main glossary text consists of 1400 entries with references to the plate illustrations, of the different forms of furniture, also its parts, woods, construction, styles, periods and famous craftsmen. These include over 170 thumbnail sketches covering all the major furniture styles and cabinetmakers—illustrated by over 100 concise line drawings of their typical pieces.

The reader should note that each entry in the glossary text will provide the category within which the object is illustrated: ie a **Bergère** is an armchair and the reader is directed to plate 1.05—the first plate showing chairs in alphabetical order. Entries for **Box bed**, **box settle**, **box stool** and **box stretcher**, can all be found under **Box**. Here they are cross referred to the plates on beds, sofas, chairs and chair construction respectively.

In addition, the chronology of the styles of furniture history is graphically clarified by a timechart, which not only shows the duration of the great styles but also demonstrates how they spread to ten different countries or regions at various times in differing sequences.

Contents

PLATE LIST

SECTION 1: OBJECTS

SECTION 2: CONSTRUCTION AND PARTS

SECTION 3: DECORATION AND FINISH

Note: The drawings on the plates are not drawn to a common scale.

1.01

OBJECTS
BEDS 1

1 Alcove
2 Angel/Lit à la duchesse
3 Bassinet
4 Box
5 Brass
6 Bureau bedstead
7 Campaign/Field
8 Camp bed (folding)
9 Chaise longue
10 Cot

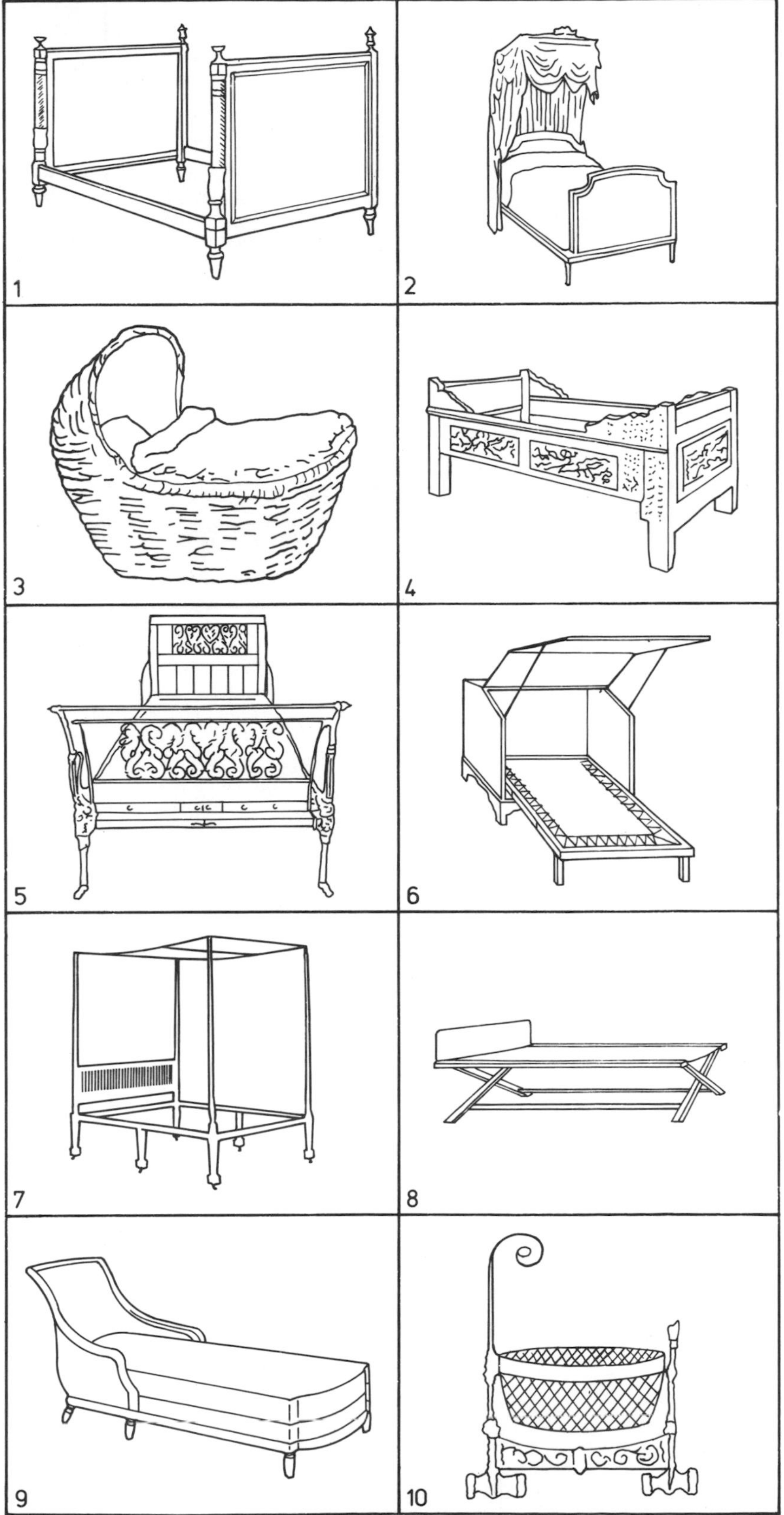

1.02 OBJECTS BEDS 2

1 Couch
2 Couchette
3 Cradle
4 Crib
5 Cupboard (Press bedstead)
6 Day bed
7 Divan
8 Dome bed
9 Folding chair bed
10 Four poster

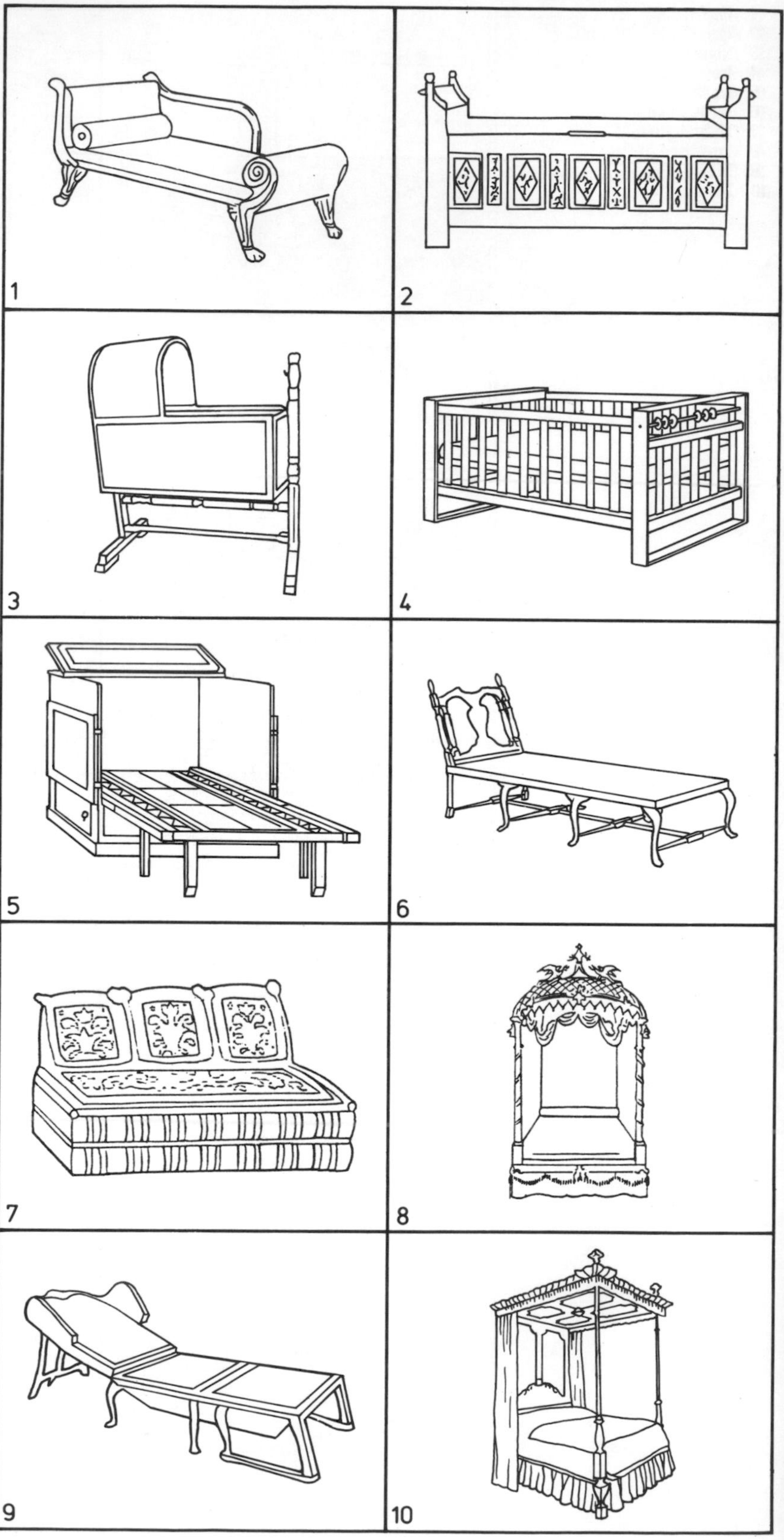

1.03

OBJECTS
BEDS 3

1 Half tester
2 Half tester (folding)
3 Kline
4 Lit à colonnes
5 Lit à la Polonaise
6 Lit de repos
7 Lit en bateau
8 Low post bed
9 Méridienne
10 Platform

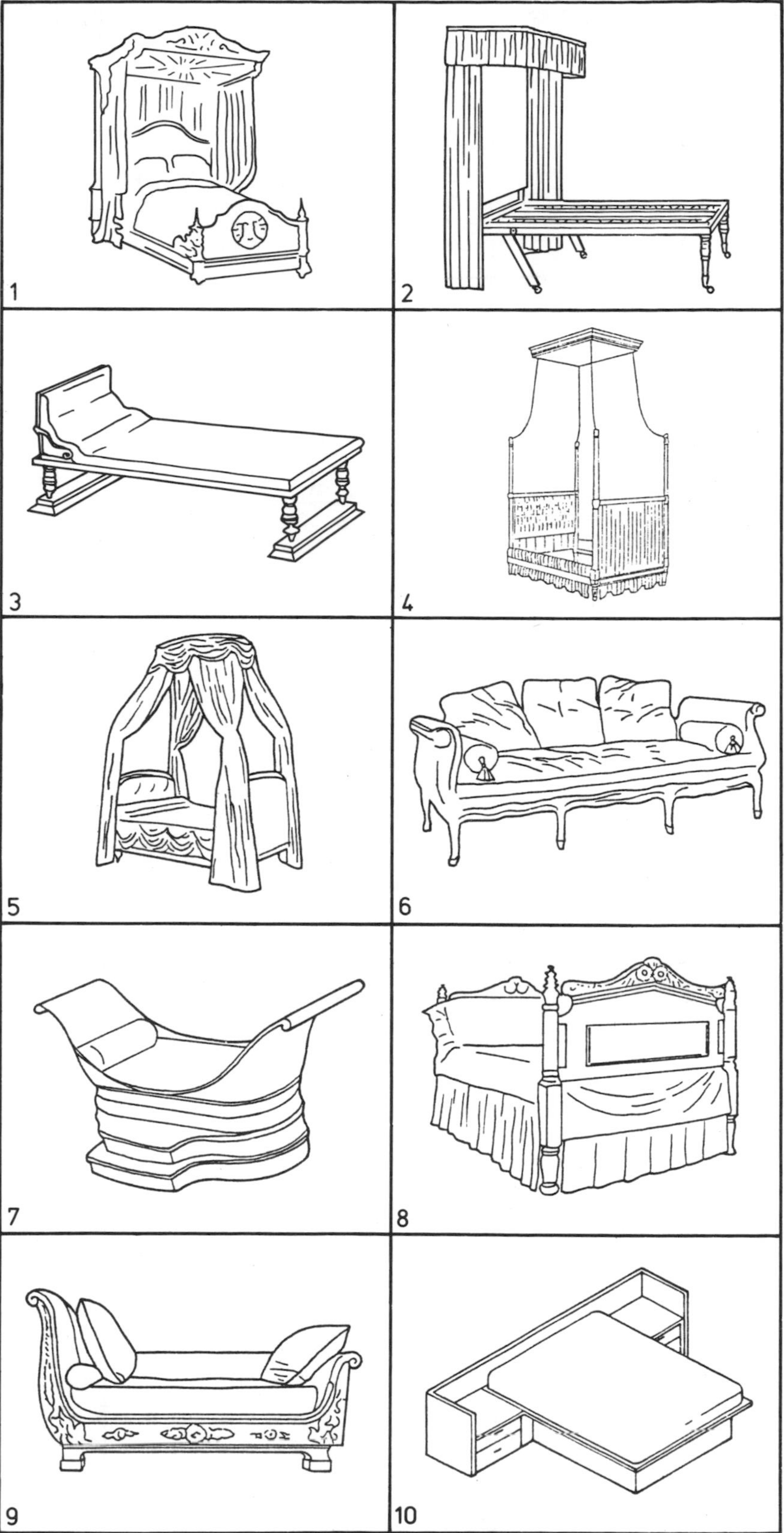

1.04 OBJECTS
BEDS 4

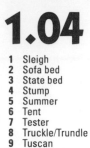

1 Sleigh
2 Sofa bed
3 State bed
4 Stump
5 Summer
6 Tent
7 Tester
8 Truckle/Trundle
9 Tuscan
10 Waterbed

1.05

OBJECTS
CHAIRS 1

1 Anthemion back
2 Arm chair
3 Back stool
4 Balloon back
5 Banister back
6 Banquette stool
7 Basket
8 Bench
9 Bentwood/Thonet No 14
10 Bergère (Chippendale Burjar)
11 Boston rocker
12 Box
13 Box stool
14 Brewster
15 Byzantine

1.06 OBJECTS CHAIRS 2

1 Cabriole
2 Cantilever
3 Caqueteuse/Caquetoire/ Conversation chair
4 Carver
5 Chair table
6 Chaise à la Capucine (rustic chair)
7 Chaise à la officier (officer's chair)
8 Chaise Courante (portable chair)
9 Chaise Meublante (heavy chair)
10 Chamber/Commode/ Necessary/Close stool
11 Chamber horse
12 Charles II/Restoration
13 Chiavari
14 Chauffeuse

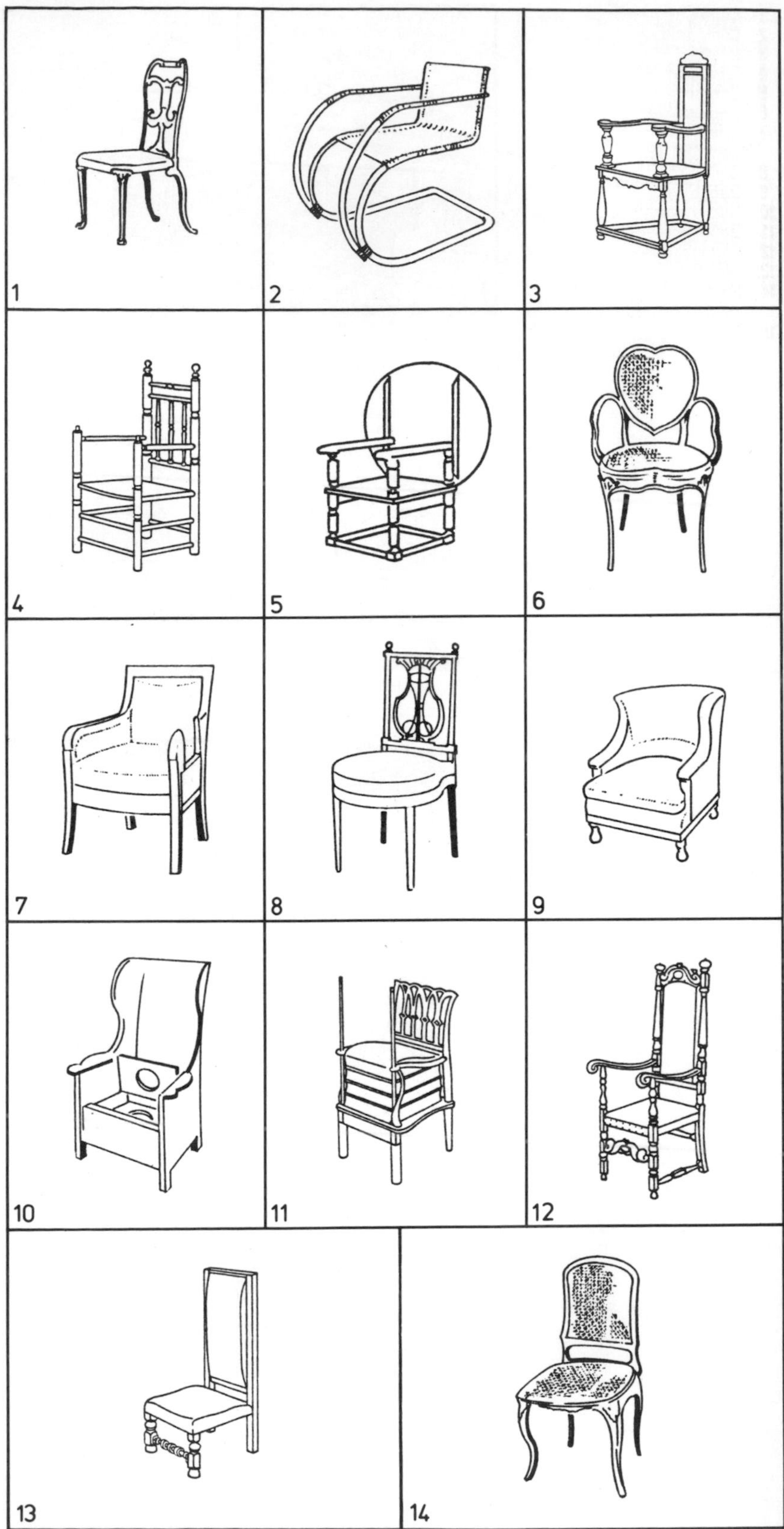

1.07

OBJECTS
CHAIRS 3

1 Coiffeuse
2 Companion
3 Confessional
4 Confortable (lounge chair)
5 Corner
6 Crapaud
7 Cromwellian/ Commonwealth
8 Curule chair
9 Dagobert
10 Deck chair
11 Desk
12 Dining
13 Diphros
14 Diphros okladias (camp folding stool)
15 Director's chair

1.08 OBJECTS CHAIRS 4

1 Directory
2 Drawing room
3 Drunkard's
4 Eames
5 Easy
6 Escabelle
8 Faldstool/medieval folding chair
9 Farthingale
10 Fauteuil (French armchair)
11 Fauteuil à la reine
12 Fauteuil de cabinet (desk armchair)
13 Fiddle/Vase back chair
14 Foot stool
15 Glastonbury

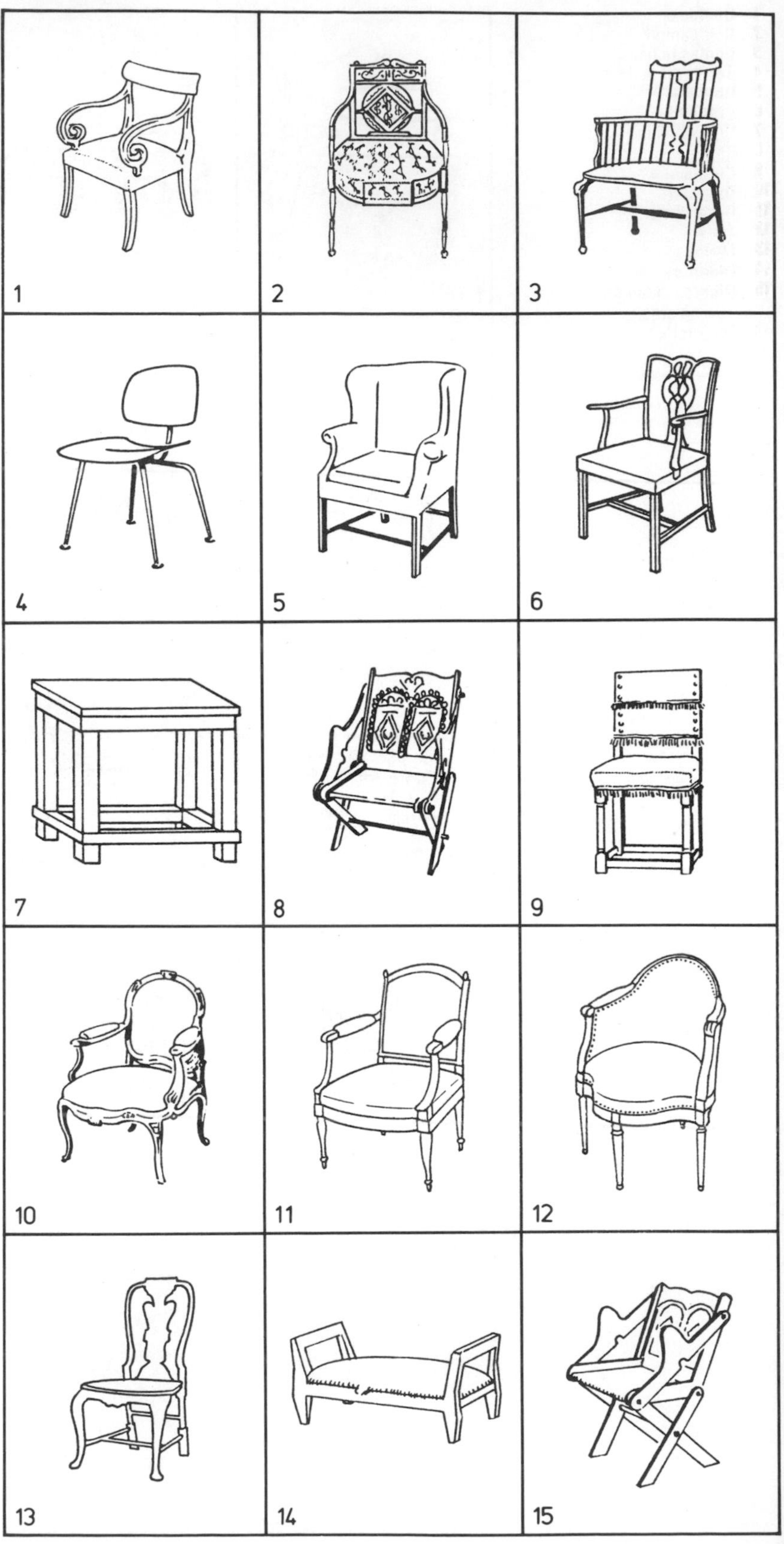

1.09

OBJECTS
CHAIRS 5

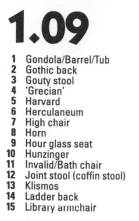

1 Gondola/Barrel/Tub
2 Gothic back
3 Gouty stool
4 'Grecian'
5 Harvard
6 Herculaneum
7 High chair
8 Horn
9 Hour glass seat
10 Hunzinger
11 Invalid/Bath chair
12 Joint stool (coffin stool)
13 Klismos
14 Ladder back
15 Library armchair

1.10

OBJECTS
CHAIRS 6

1 Lolling back
2 Lyre back
3 Marquise
4 Martha Washington
5 Misericord
6 Mission
7 Morris
8 Nursery
9 Oval back
10 Parlour
11 Pedestal
12 Pew
13 Piano stool
14 Placet
15 Platform rocker

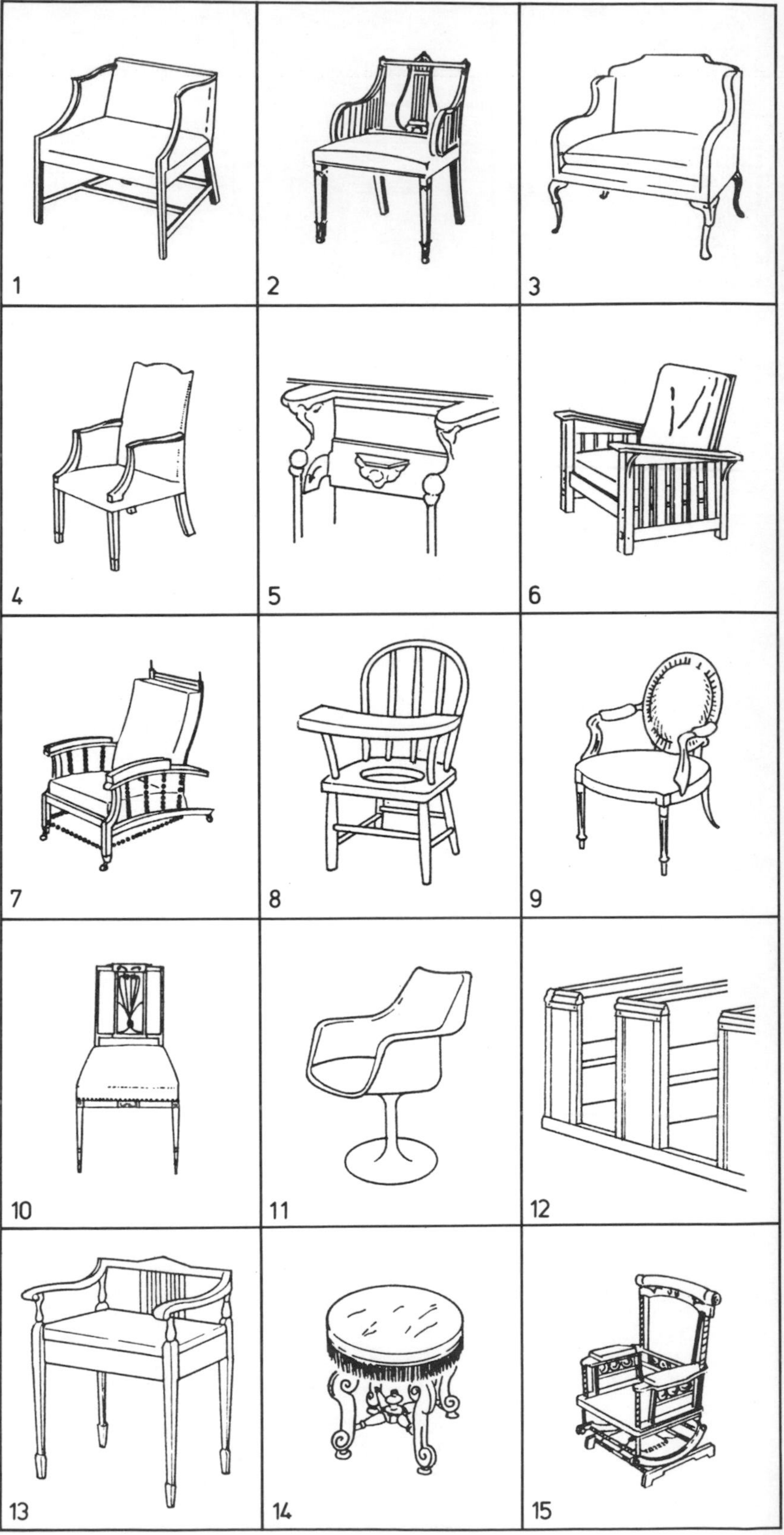

1.11

OBJECTS
CHAIRS 7

1 Pouf
2 Porter's chair
3 Prie-dieu
4 Reading chair
5 Revolving chair
6 Ribband back
7 Rocking
8 Roundabout (burgomaster)
9 Roundback/Quaker
10 Rustic
11 Scroll back
12 Sedan
13 Sella curulis
14 Sgabello/Board
15 Shaker

1.12

OBJECTS
CHAIRS 8

1 Shaving chair
2 Sheaf back
3 Shield back
4 Side
5 Sillón de fraileros
6 Slab-ended stool
7 Sleeping
8 Slipper
9 Spindle back
10 Spoon back
11 Square back
12 Steamer
13 Step ladder
14 Stick/Cricket/Milking stool
15 Straw chair (beehive type)

1.13

OBJECTS
CHAIRS 9

1 Tabouret/Taboret
2 Tasselback
3 Throne (box-seated)
4 Tulip
5 Turned/'Thrown'
6 Vienna
7 Voyeuse (conversation chair)
8 Wainscot
9 Wheel
10 Wicker
11 Wing/Grandfather
12 Writing
13 X-frame (German Luther, Italian Dante or Savonarola, Spanish sillón de cadera)
14 Yorkshire
15 Zanzibar

1.14

OBJECTS
WINDSOR CHAIRS 1

1 Arrow back (US only)
2 Balloon back
3 Bergère back
4 Bow back/Loop back/ Single bow back
5 Buckle back
6 Captain's
7 Comb back
8 Continuous arm
9 Fan back
10 Firehouse
11 Gothic scroll back
12 Gothic/Strawberry Hill/ Window Splat
13 Interlaced bow
14 Lath and baluster
15 Lath back (Wycombe style)

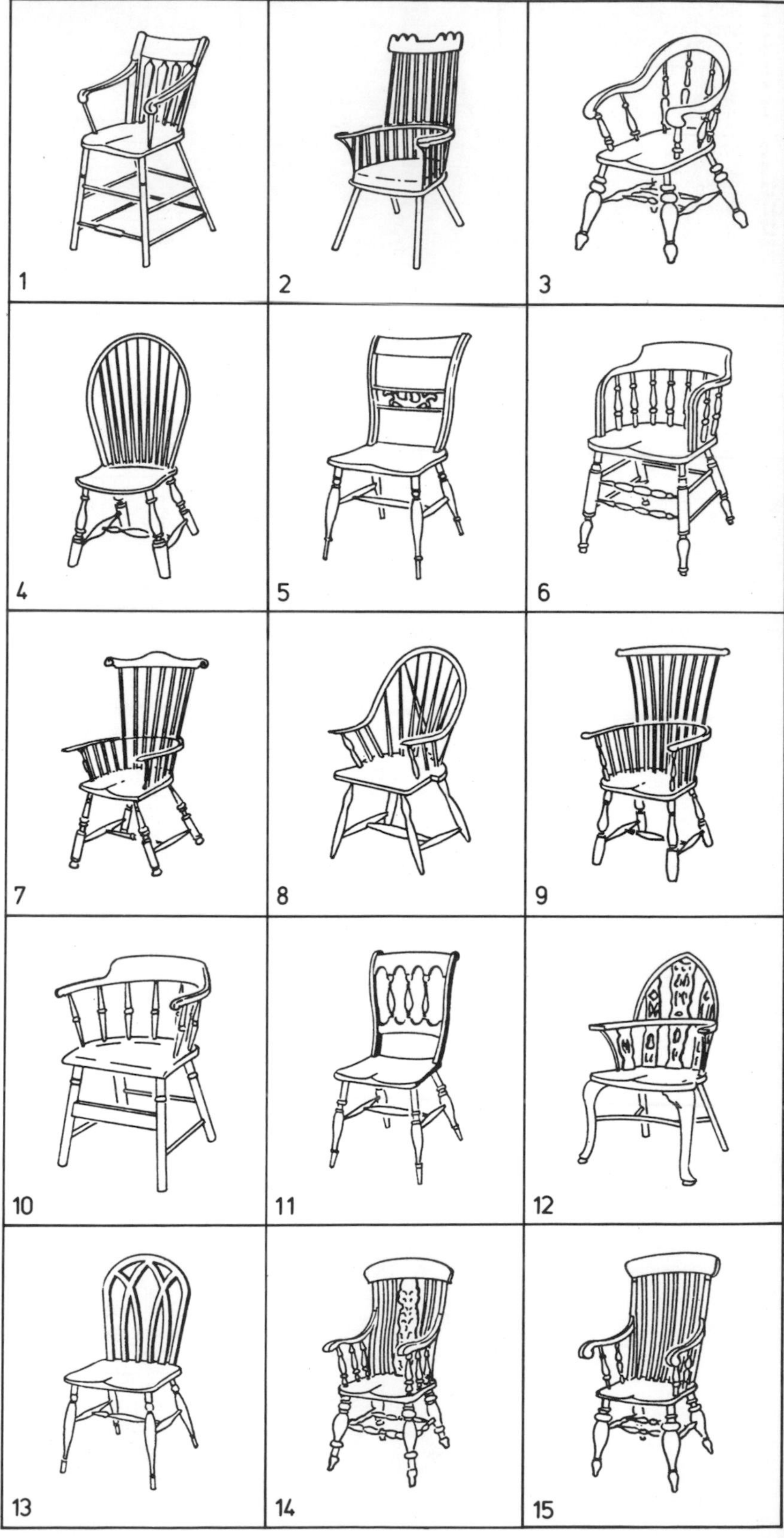

1.15

OBJECTS
WINDSOR CHAIRS 2

1 Mendlesham
2 Nelson/Trafalgar
3 Sack back (bow back)
4 Scroll back/Stay back
5 Shawl back
6 Smoker's bow
7 Spindleback (Wycombe style)
8 Swiss
9 Tablet back
10 Three back (US only)
11 Wheel back
12 Writing arm

1.16

OBJECTS
CHESTS AND BOXES 1

1 Armada
2 Bachelor's
3 Bible box
4 Blanket
5 Board
6 Bombé
7 Box
8 Bridal
9 Cassone (sarcophagus type)
10 Cassone
11 Cellaret
12 Chest of drawers
13 Chest on chest
14 Chest on stand
15 Chiffonier/Chiffonière Semainier
16 Coffre
17 Commode (à la regence)
18 Commode clothes press

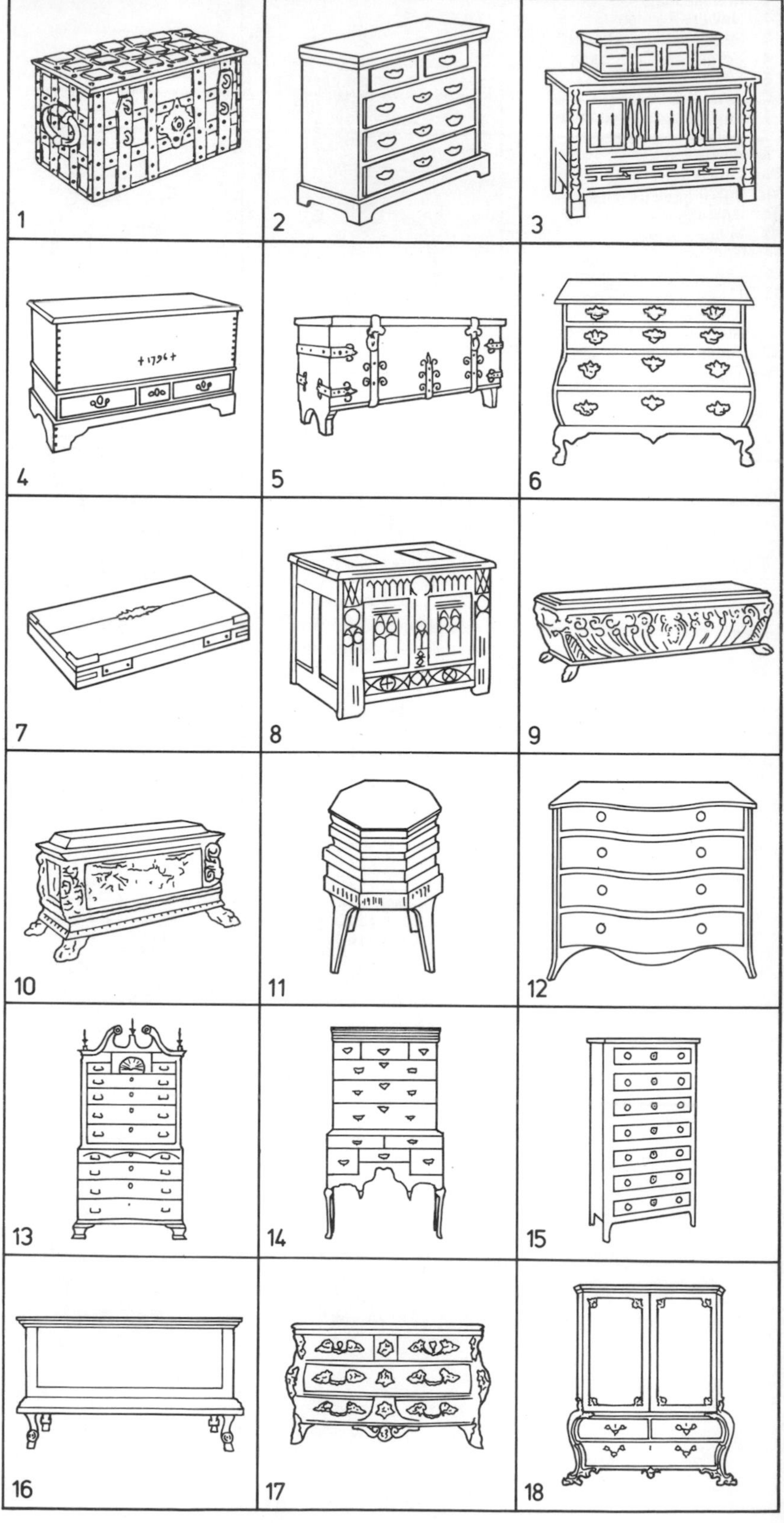

1.17

OBJECTS
CHESTS AND BOXES 2

1 Commode cressent
2 Commode table
3 Commode tombeau
4 Connecticut
5 Demilune commode
6 Desk box
7 Dower
8 Dressing
9 Guilford
10 Hadley
11 Hutch
12 Lowboy
13 Mule
14 Nonsuch
15 Sea chest
16 Tallboy/Highboy (US) (chest-on-chest with secretaire fitment)
17 Tea chest
18 Trunk

1.18 OBJECTS
CUPBOARDS 1

1 Armadio
2 Armoire
3 Armoire à deux corps
4 Beeldenkast
5 Bonnetière
6 Bookcase
7 Bureau bookcase (Secretary, US)
8 Cabinet

1.19

OBJECTS
CUPBOARDS 2

1. Cabinet-on-chest
2. Cabinet-on-stand
3. Chiffonier/Table en chiffonière
4. China cabinet
5. Coin cabinet
6. Corner cupboard
7. Corner cabinet
8. Court cupboard

1.20

OBJECTS
CUPBOARDS 3

1 Credenza
2 Dresser
3 Drinks cabinet
4 Dwarf bookcase
5 Encoignure
6 Hall cupboard/Clothes press
7 Hanging cupboard
8 Kast
9 Keeftkast
10 Kunstschrank

1.21

1 Kussenkast
2 Library bookcase
3 Music cabinet
4 Pedestal cabinet
5 Plate cupboard
6 Press cupboard
7 Print cabinet
8 Schenkschieve

OBJECTS
CUPBOARDS 4

1.22

OBJECTS
CUPBOARDS 5

1 Schrank
2 Tridarn
3 Uberauschrank
4 Vaisselier
5 Welsh dresser
6 Wing clothes press
7 Wing wardrobe
8 Writing cabinet

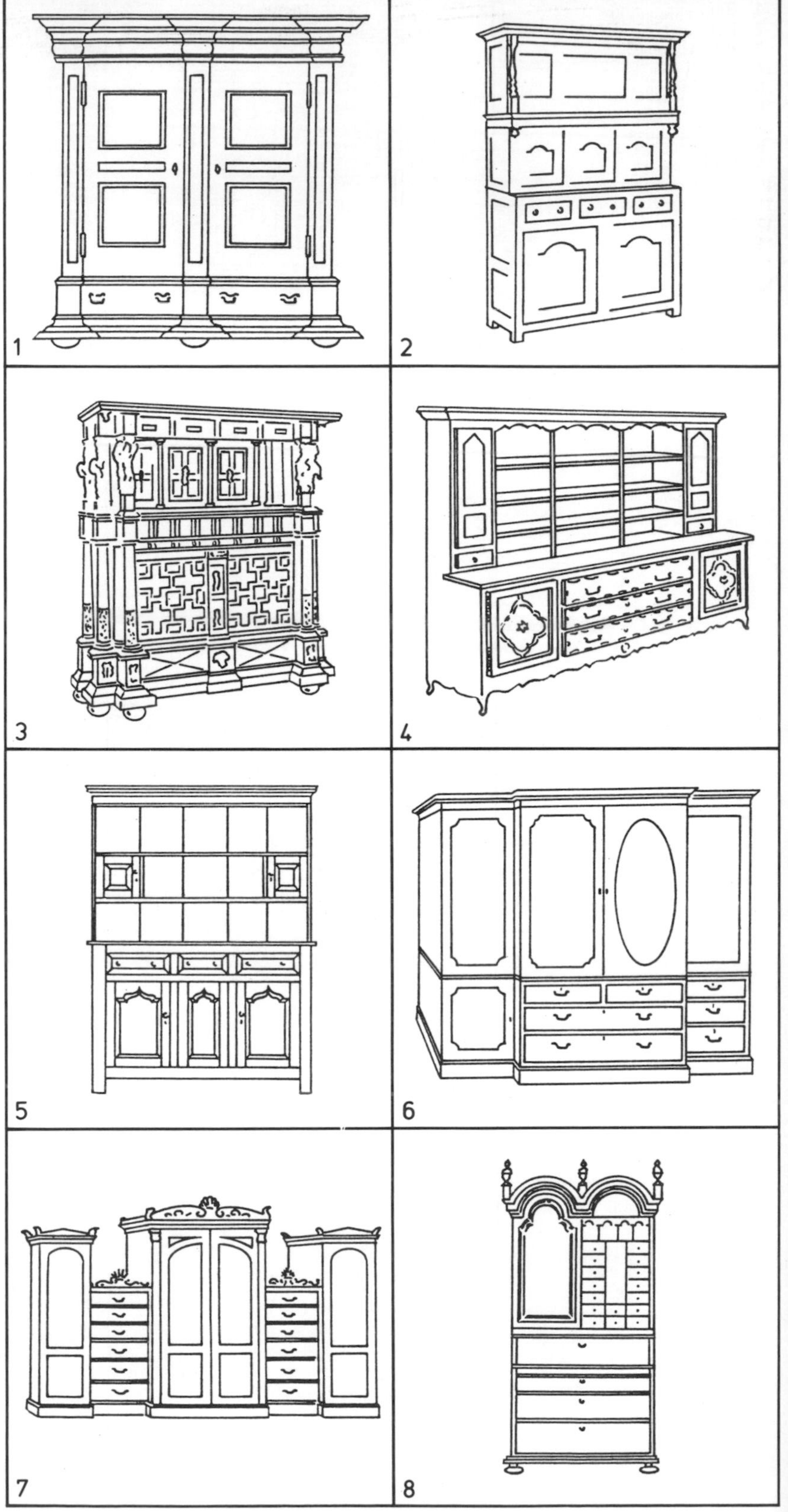

OBJECTS
DESKS AND BUREAUX 1

1 Bonheur du jour
2 Bureau
3 Bureau table
4 Chatol
5 Coaching writing desk
6 Cylinder bureau
7 Davenport
8 Drop-front desk
9 Escritoire
10 Fall-front desk
11 Kneehole desk
12 Roll top desk
13 Screen desk
14 Sheveret (cheveret)
15 Vargueño

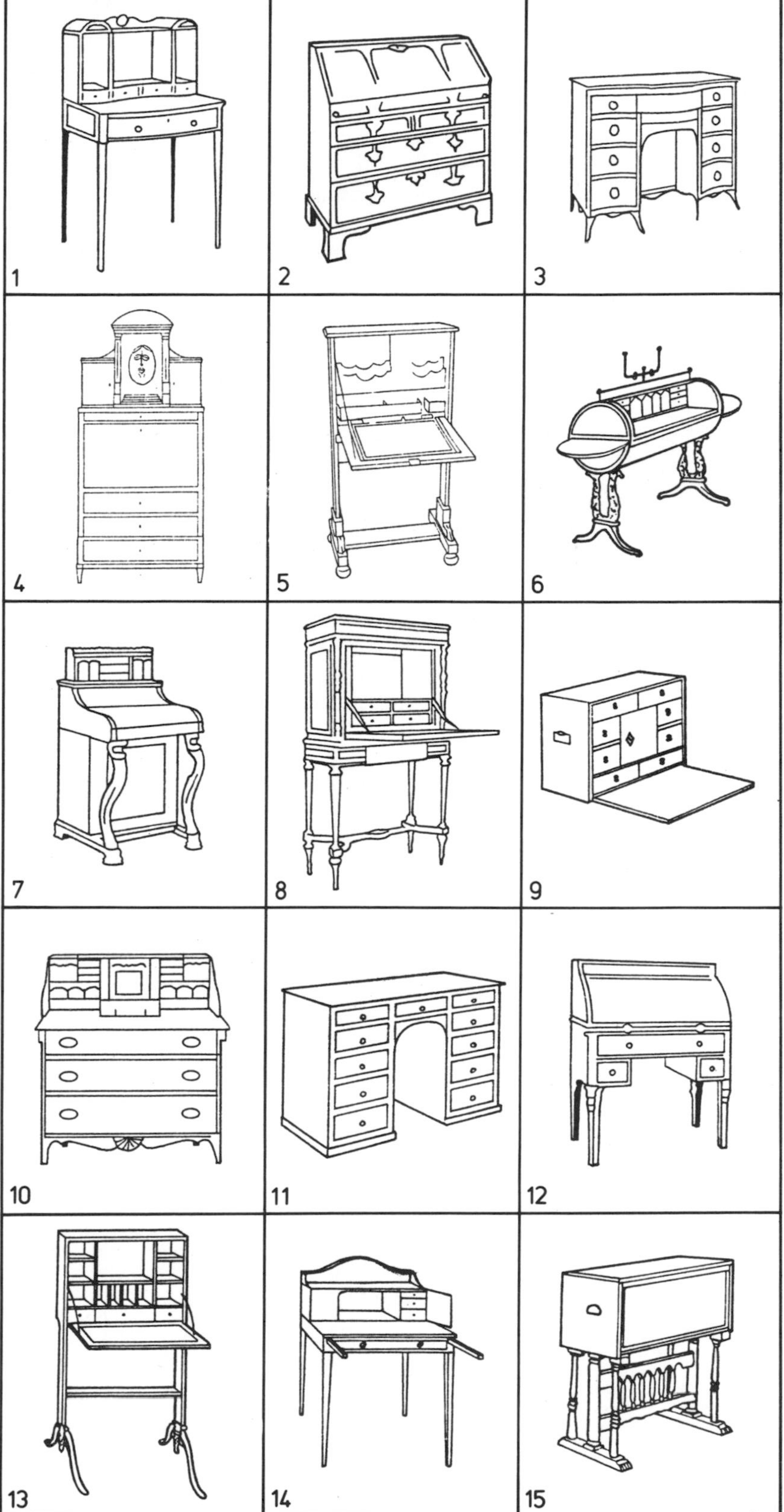

1.24

OBJECTS
DESKS AND BUREAUX 2

1 Bureau Mazarin
2 Bureau plat
3 Partner's desk
4 Pedestal desk
5 Scritoire
6 Secretary (US)/Bureau cabinet
7 Secrétaire à abattant
8 Secretaire-bookcase
9 Secrétaire commode
10 Writing box

1.25

OBJECTS
SOFAS 1

1 Assemblage
2 Banquette
3 Bar back sofa
4 Bench
5 Biedermeier sofa
6 Bisellium
7 Borne
8 Box settle
9 Cabriole sofa
10 Camel back/Humpback
11 Canapé
12 Cassapance

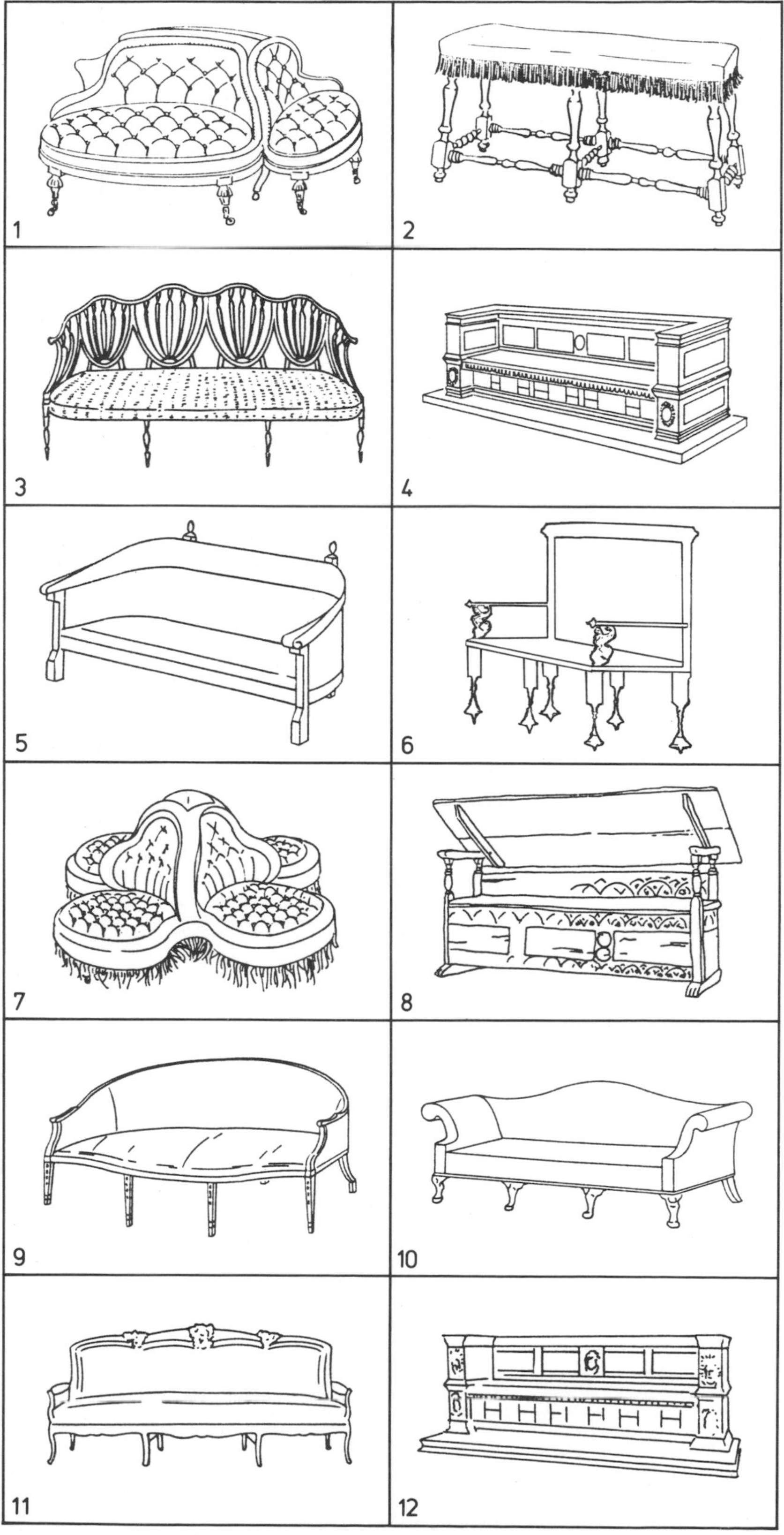

1.26

OBJECTS
SOFAS 2

1 Chair back settee (2–5 backs)
2 Chaise longue
3 Chesterfield
4 Club Sofa
5 Confidante/Ballroom sofa
6 Confidante/Companion chair
7 Corridor stool/Window seat
8 Cosy corner
9 Couch
10 Day bed
11 Duchesse brisée
12 Duchesse en bateau

1.27

OBJECTS
SOFAS 3

1 French corner chair
2 Grecian couch
3 Hall settee
4 Indiscret
5 Kangaroo sofa
6 Love seat/Courting chair
7 Méridienne
8 Ottoman
9 Papier-mâché settee
10 Reading seat

1.28

OBJECTS
SOFAS 4

1 Récamier
2 Rest bed
3 Settee (Windsor)
4 Settle (low back)
5 Settle (high back)
6 Sociable
7 Sofa
8 Vis-à-vis/Tête-à-tête/ Siamoise
9 Wagon seat
10 Windsor settee/Double Windsor

1.29

OBJECTS
STANDS 1

1 Anthenienne
2 Basin stand
3 Basket stand
4 Book stand
5 Candle stand
6 Corner basin stand
7 Dressing stand
8 Dressing/Toilet glass
9 Dumb waiter/Lazy Susan (US)
10 Flower stand/Jardinière
11 Guéridon
12 Hat/Hall stand
13 Lamp stand
14 Globe stand
15 Magazine rack
16 Music Canterbury

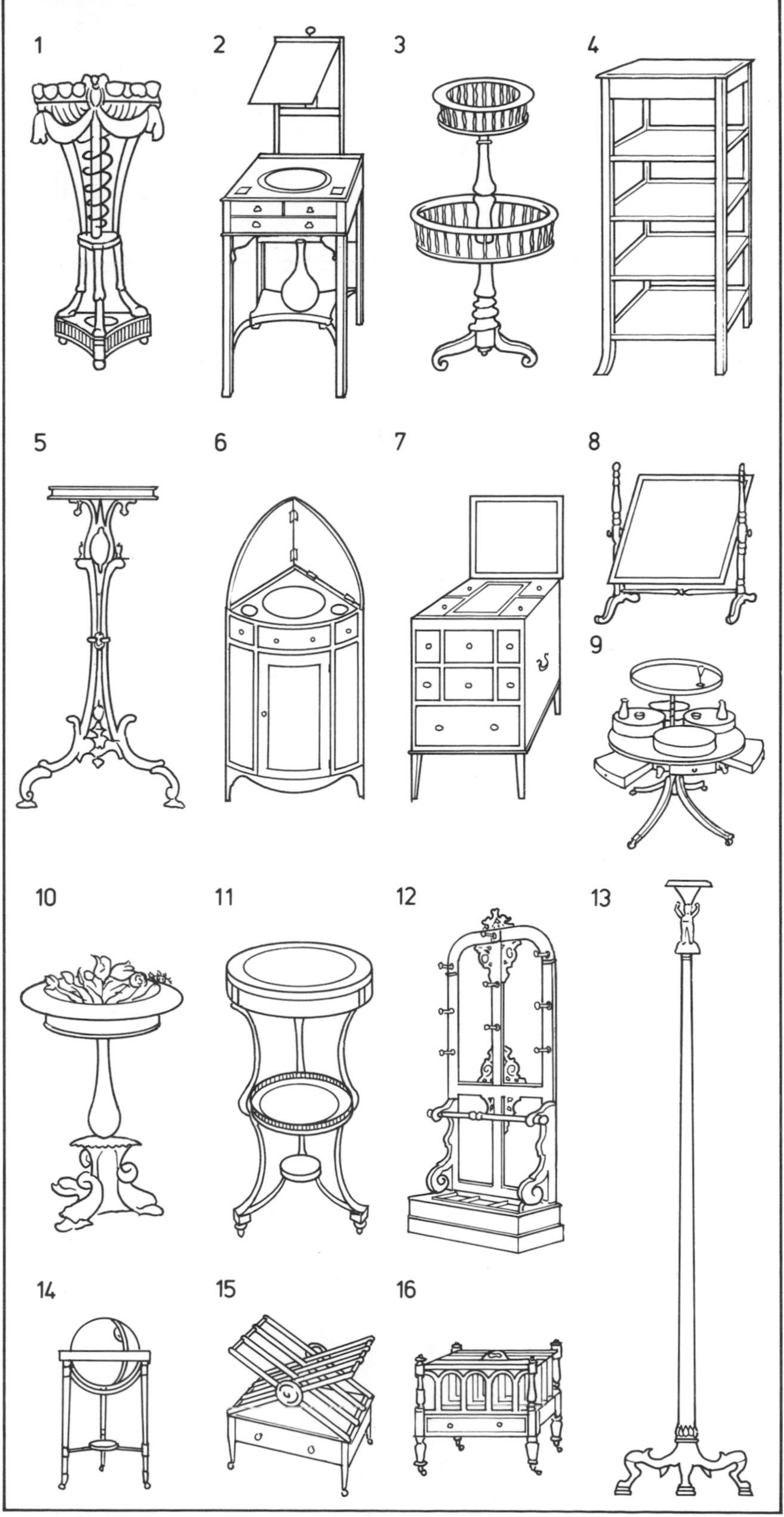

1.30

OBJECTS
STANDS 2

1 Lectern
2 Music stand
3 Pedestal (for sideboard)
4 Pulpit
5 Plant stand
6 Portfolio stand
7 Pot table
8 Supper Canterbury
9 Revolving bookcase
10 Shaving stand
11 Tea kettle stand
12 Term
13 Umbrella stand
14 'Wig stand' (basin stand)
15 Wash hand stand
16 Whatnot/Étagère
17 Wine cooler
18 Work stand

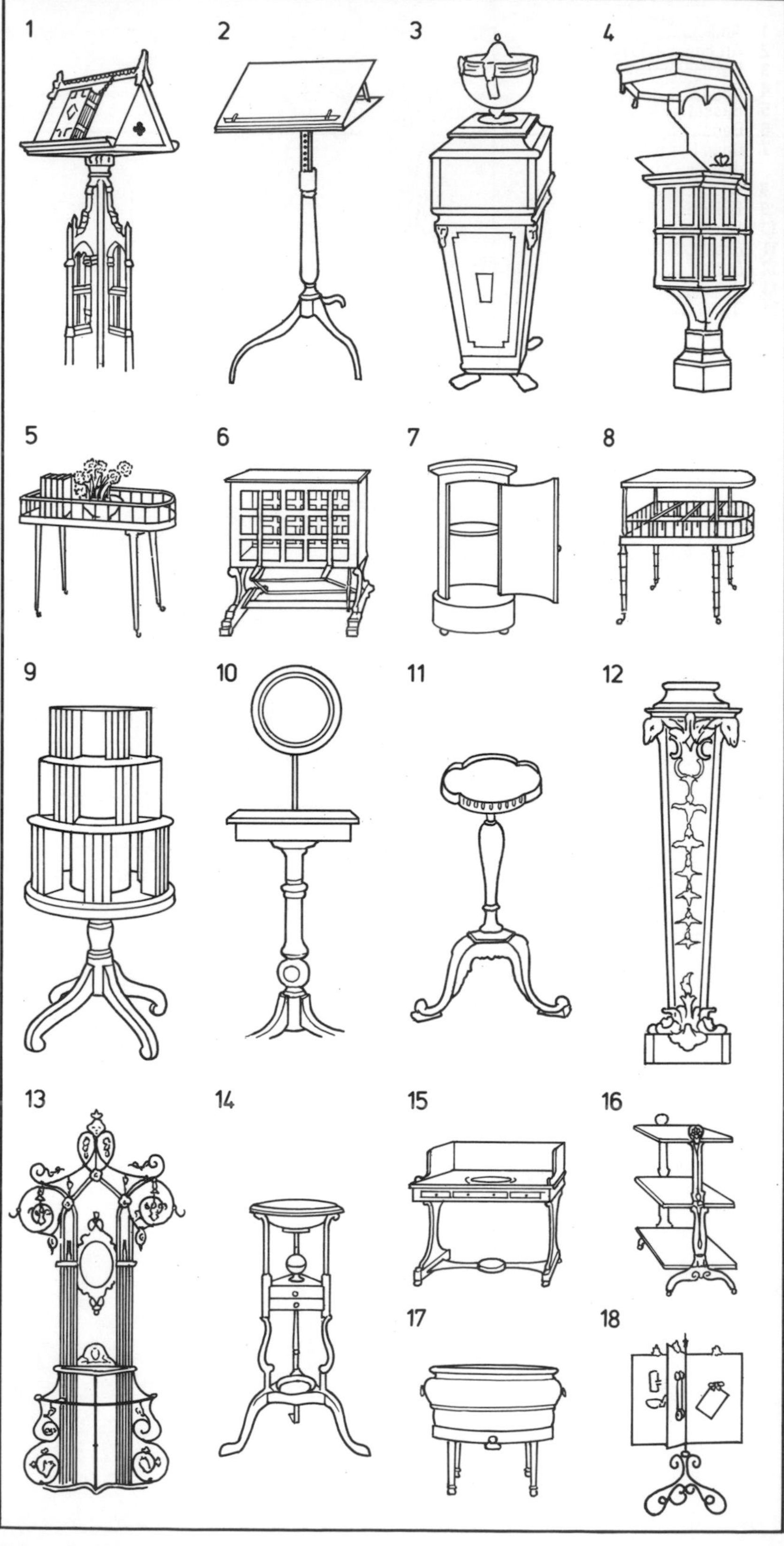

1.31

OBJECTS
TABLES 1

1 Ambulante
2 Architect's table
3 Backgammon table
4 Bag table
5 Basset table/Card table
6 Bench table
7 Beau Brummel/Rudd's dressing table
8 Bijouterie
9 Billiard table
10 Bouillotte table
11 Breakfast table
12 Buffet
13 Bureau plat
14 Butler's table/tray

1.32

OBJECTS
TABLES 2

1 Butterfly table
2 Cabinet stand
3 Canterbury
4 Card table
5 Chess table (sofa type)
6 Carlton House table
7 China table
8 Coffee table
9 Coiffeuse
10 Console desserte
11 Console table
12 Credence

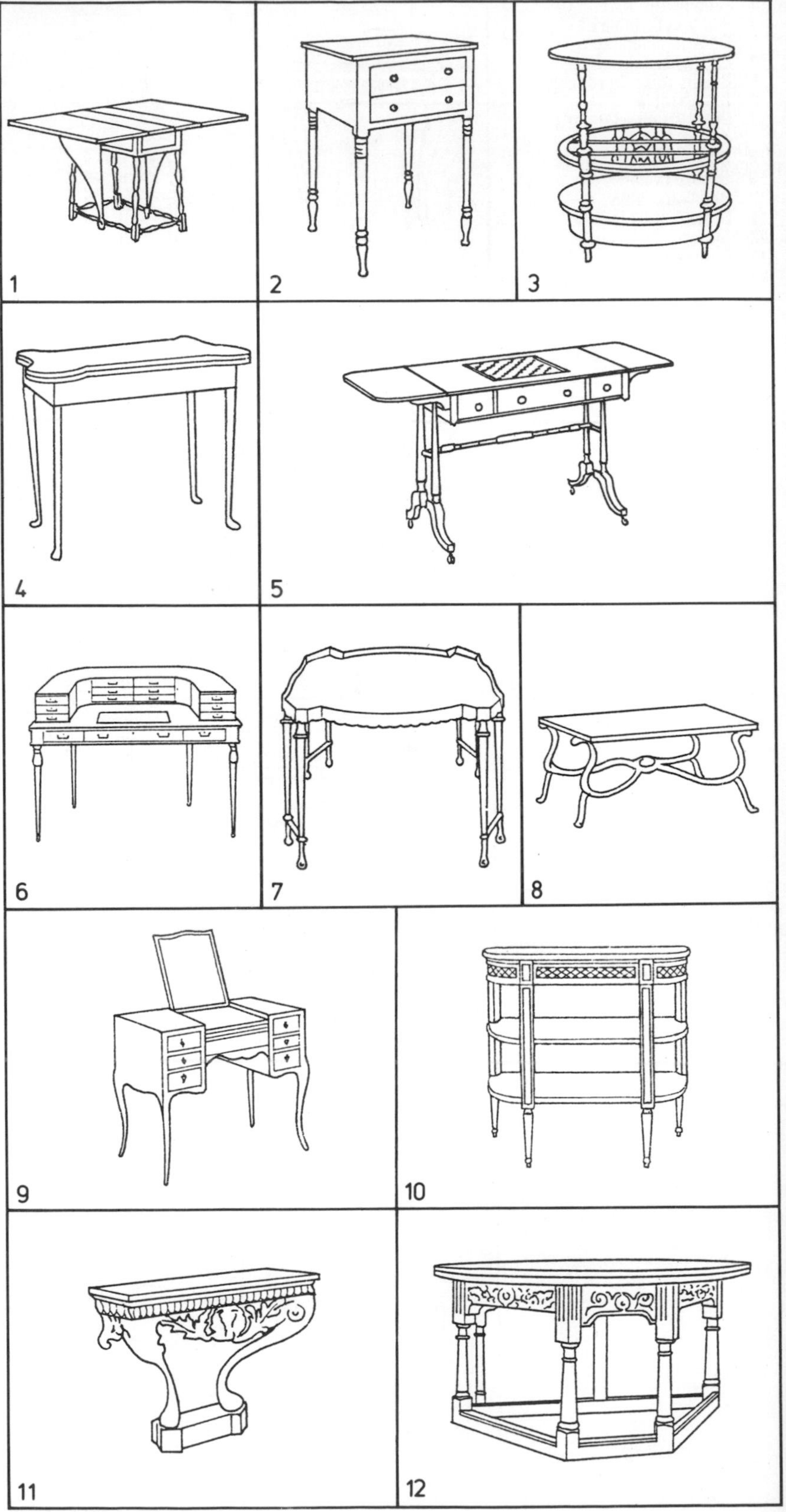

1.33 OBJECTS
TABLES 3

1 Credenza
2 Cricket table
3 Dining table
4 Deception table
5 Draw leaf table
6 Dressing table/Poudreuse
7 Drinking table
8 Drum table
9 Drop leaf table
10 Eagle table

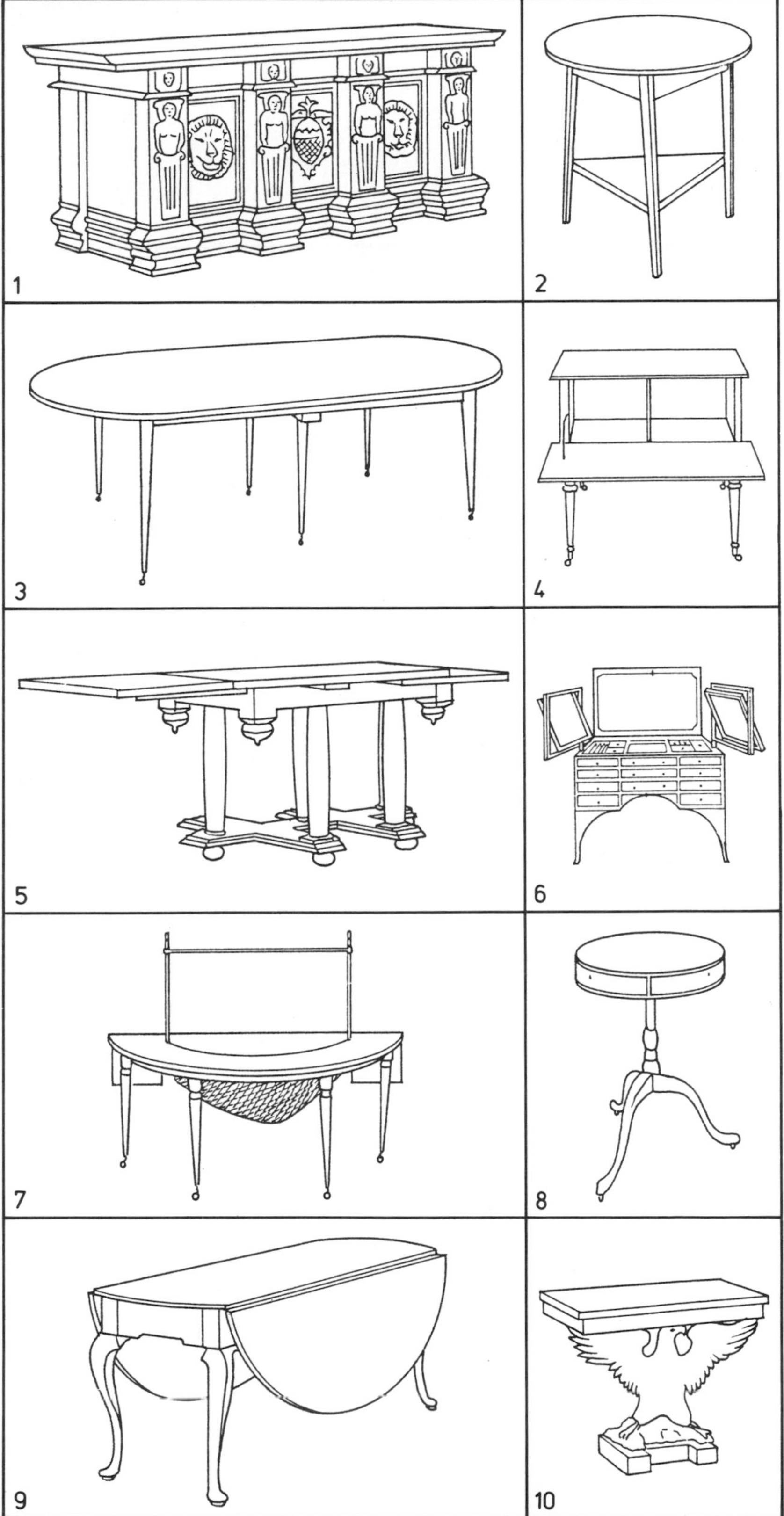

OBJECTS
TABLES 4

1 Extension table
2 Gaming table
3 Gate leg table
4 Guard room table
5 Handkerchief table
6 Harlequin table
7 Horseshoe dining table
8 Horseshoe writing (kidney) table
9 Hunt board
10 Hunt table

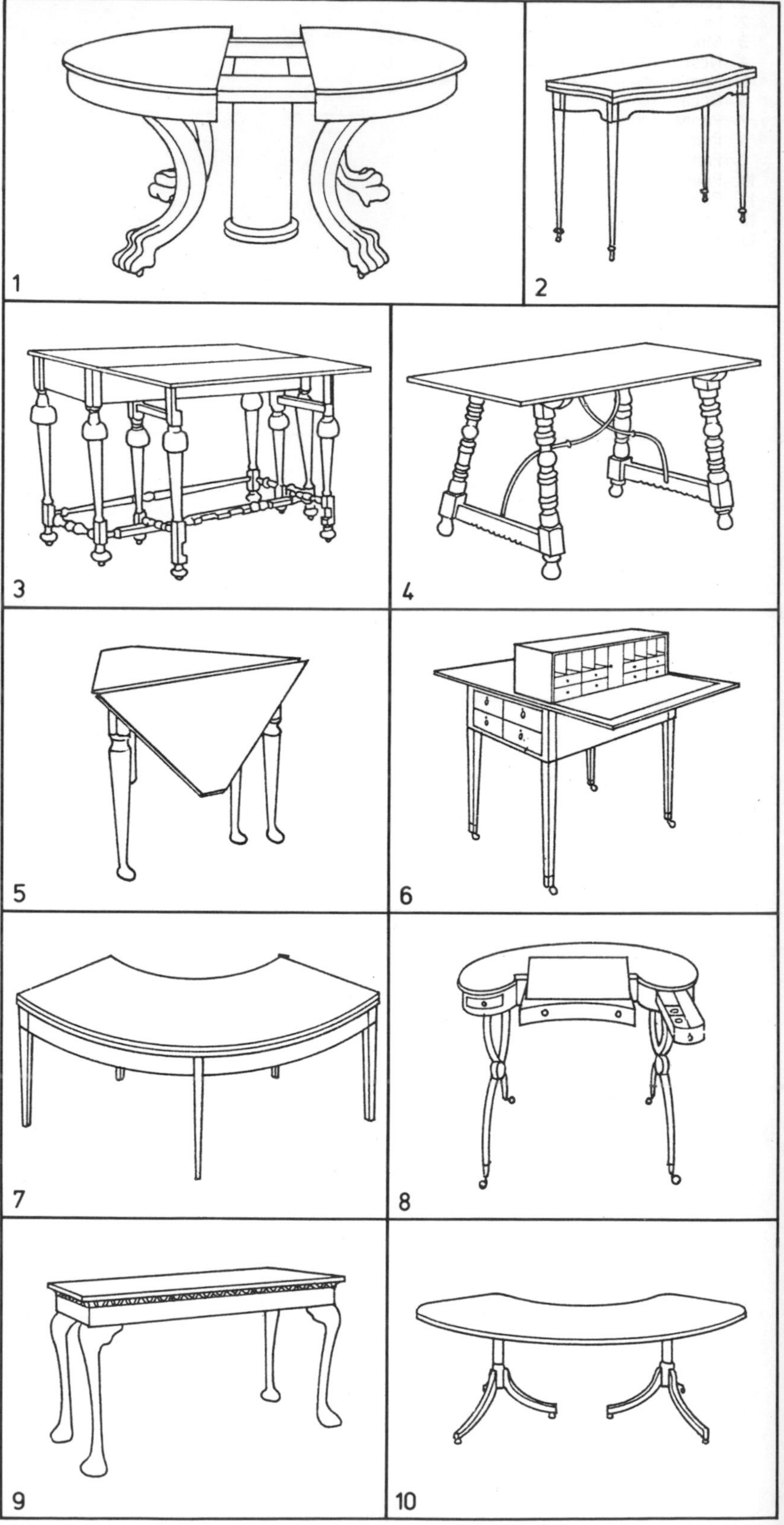

1.35

OBJECTS
TABLES 5

1 Library table
2 Loo table
3 Mixing table
4 Nest of tables (trio)
5 Nest of tables (quartetto)
6 Occasional table
7 Pedestal table
8 Pembroke table
9 Pier table
10 Pouch table
11 Rent table
12 Refectory table
13 Rudd/Lady's dressing table

1.36

OBJECTS
TABLES 6

1 Schragentisch
2 Sewing table
3 Sewing machine table
4 Shaving table
5 Sideboard
6 Social table
7 Sofa table
8 Specimen table
9 Stand
10 Table à l'Italienne
11 Table à rognon
12 Table en chiffonière
13 Tavern table

1.37 OBJECTS TABLES 7

1 Teapoy
2 Tea table
3 Tilt top table
4 Toilette en papillon
5 Toylet table (Toiletta)
6 Tricoteuse
7 Trestle table
8 Tric trac
9 Tripod table
10 Troumadam
11 Vitrine table
12 Wine table and stand
13 Writing table/Table à ecrire

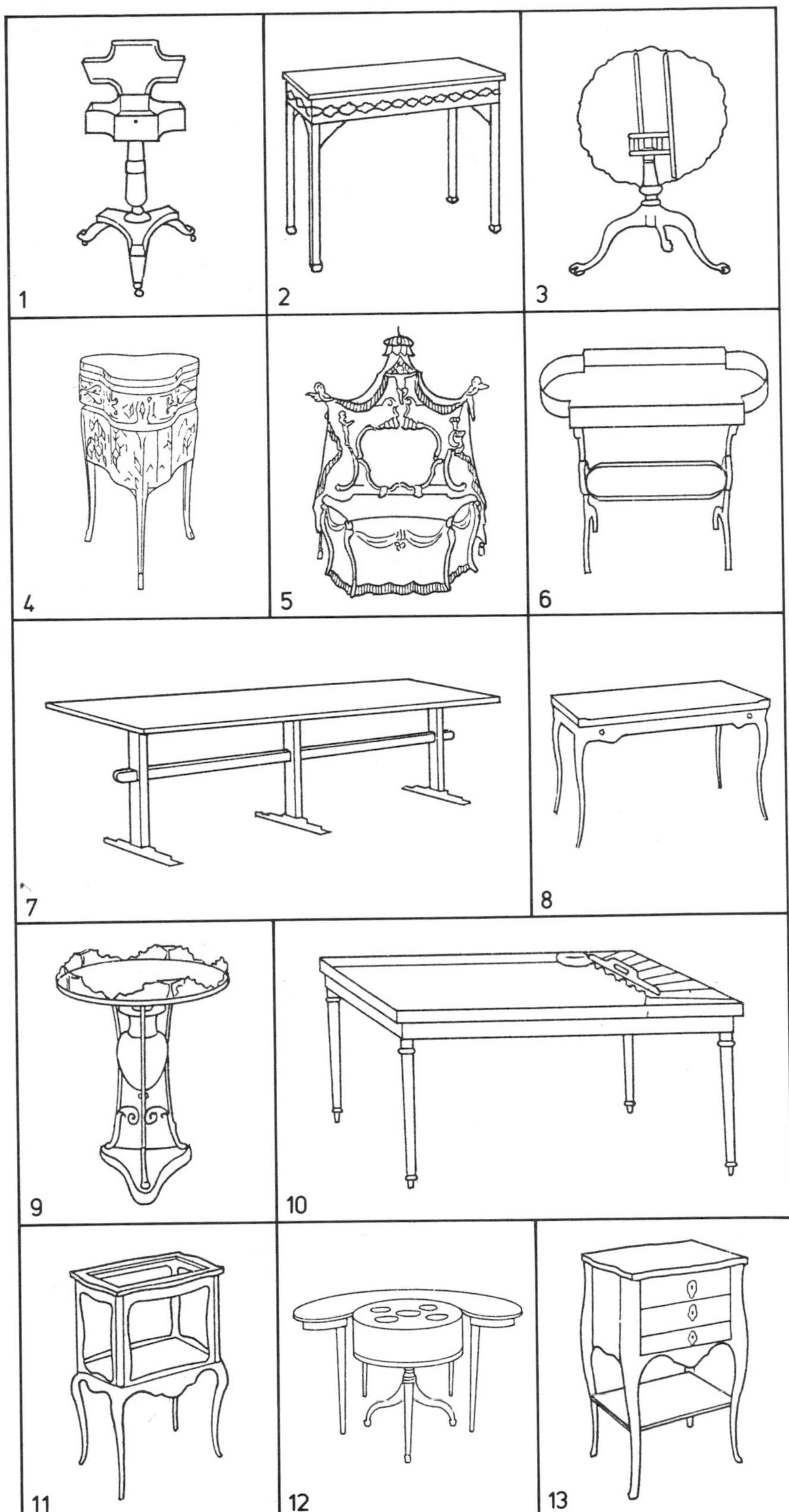

1.38

OBJECTS
OTHER FURNITURE 1

1 Betty lamp
2 Candelabrum
3 Girandole
4 Tripod light
5 Andiron/Fire dog
6 Candlestick
7 Chandelier
8 Cresset
9 Crusie (hanging oil lamp)
10 Moon
11 Purdonium/Purdonian
12 Sconce
13 Stove grate
14 Gentlemen's writing screen
15 Ladies' writing screen
16 Library screen
17 Horse fire screen
18 Pole screen
19 Tripod screen
20 Sliding screen
21 Sliding and swinging screen

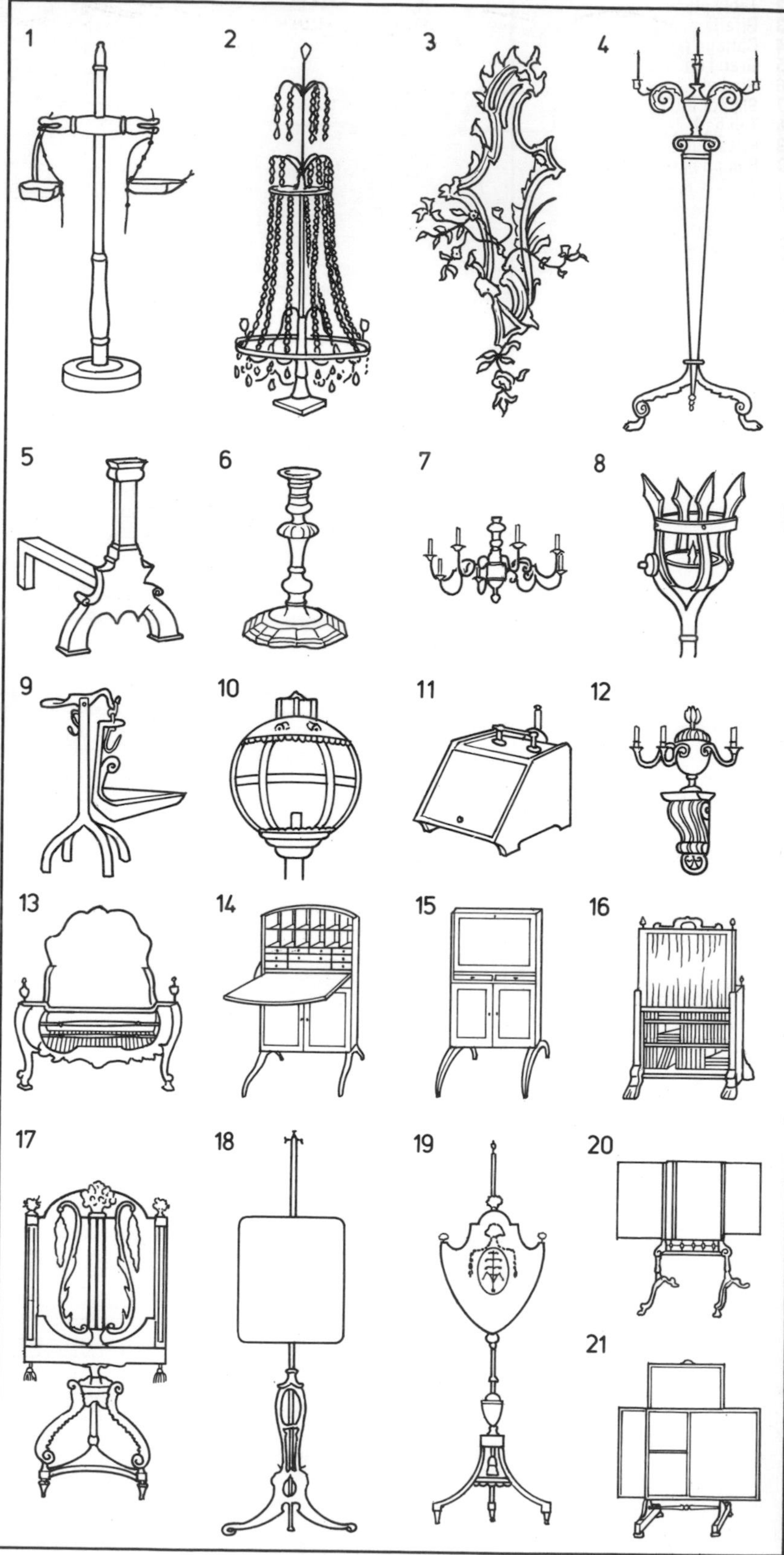

1.39

OBJECTS
OTHER FURNITURE 2

1 Spinet
2 Table piano
3 Giraffe piano
4 Cottage piano
5 Grand cottage piano
6 Hip bath
7 Slipper bath
8 Tub bath
9 Kneading trough
10 Roman bath

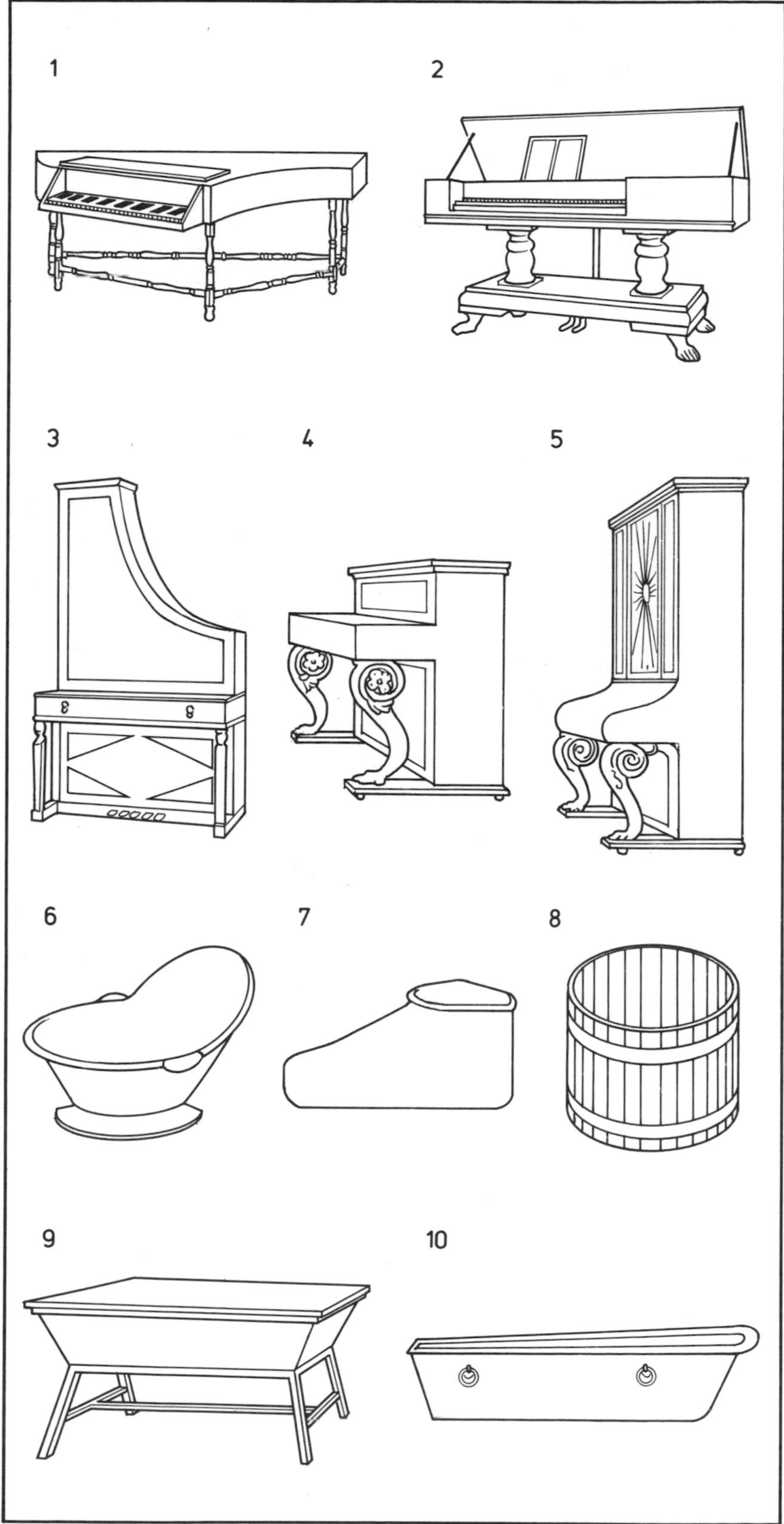

1.40 OBJECTS
OTHER FURNITURE 3

1 Hanging shelves
2 Tabernacle frame
3 Cheval glass
4 Dressing mirror
5 Mirror
6 Pelmet
7 Trumeau
8 Library steps
9 Candle box
10 Shelf cluster
11 Bed steps
12 Leg rest
13 Linen/Card press
14 Screen
15 Jardinière
16 Prie dieu

2.01

CONSTRUCTION AND PARTS
BED CONSTRUCTION

A

Parts of bedstead

1 Leg
2 Bedstead bolt
3 End rail
4 Footboard (bedstock)
5 Slat
6 Side rail
7 Headboard (bedstock)
8 Bedpost
9 Valance
10 Half tester
11 Canopy
12 Headboard panel

B **Types of bedstead**
13 Stump
14 Stump end
15 Brass
16 Half tester
17 Tester
18 Four poster

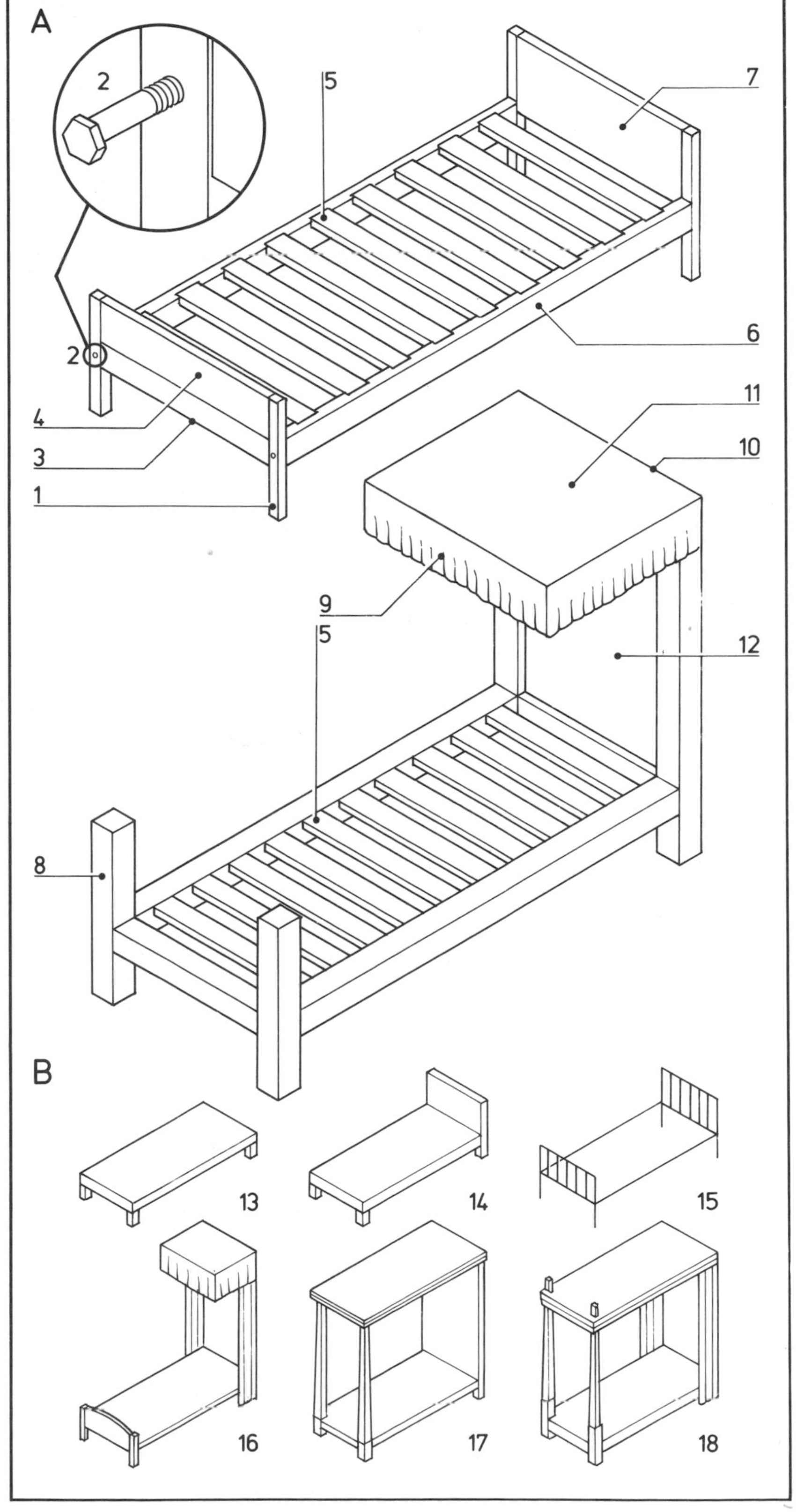

2.02

CONSTRUCTION AND PARTS
CHAIR CONSTRUCTION 1

A Chair parts
1 Top rail
2 Back rest
3 Backpost (stile)
4 Seat rail
5 Lambrequin
6 Leg
7 Side stretcher
8 Tailpiece
9 Cross rail (span, slat)
10 Arm pad
11 Arm rail
12 Arm stump
13 Corner block
14 Apron
15 Footrail
16 Cross stretcher
17 Bow top (back rest)
18 Splat (back rest)
19 Baluster/Spindle (back rest)
20 Upholstered (back rest)

B Arms
21 Bolster
22 Rollover
23 Scroll
24 Scrollover
25 Writing
26 Ram's horn

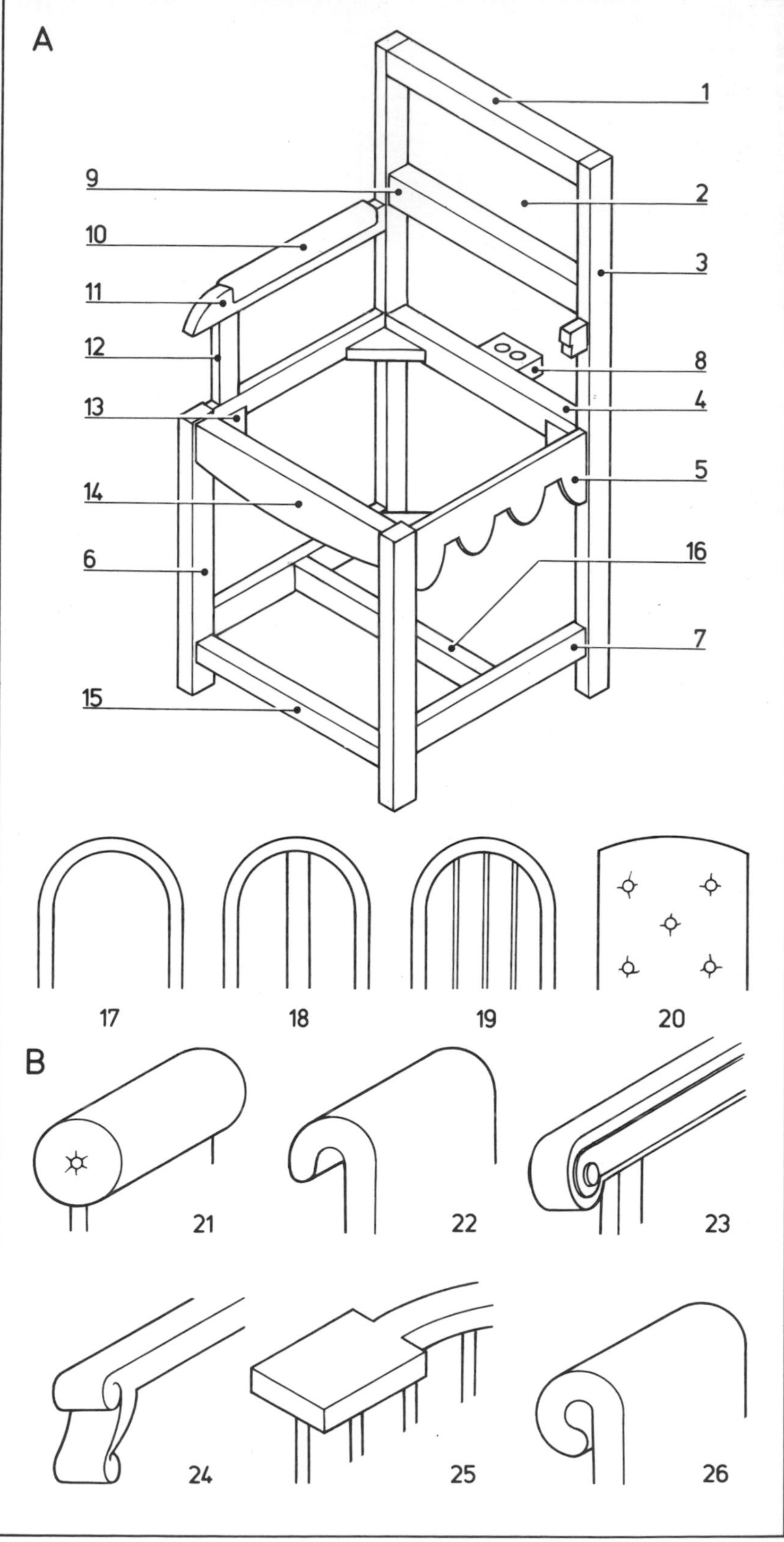

2.03

CONSTRUCTION AND PARTS
CHAIR CONSTRUCTION 2

C Seats
27 Cheesebox
28 Dropped/Scoop
29 Slip/Loose
30 Upholstered
31 Tape
32 Rush
33 Plank
34 Splint

D Stretchers
35 Recessed (black)
36 Rising
37 Runner
38 Pierced cross
39 X-shape (cross)
40 H-stretcher
41 Bent (box)
42 Sledge
43 Serpentine
44 Cowhorn/Spur/Crescent/ Crinoline
45 Double cowhorn
46 Saltire
47 Arched
48 Double lyre
49 Isle of Man

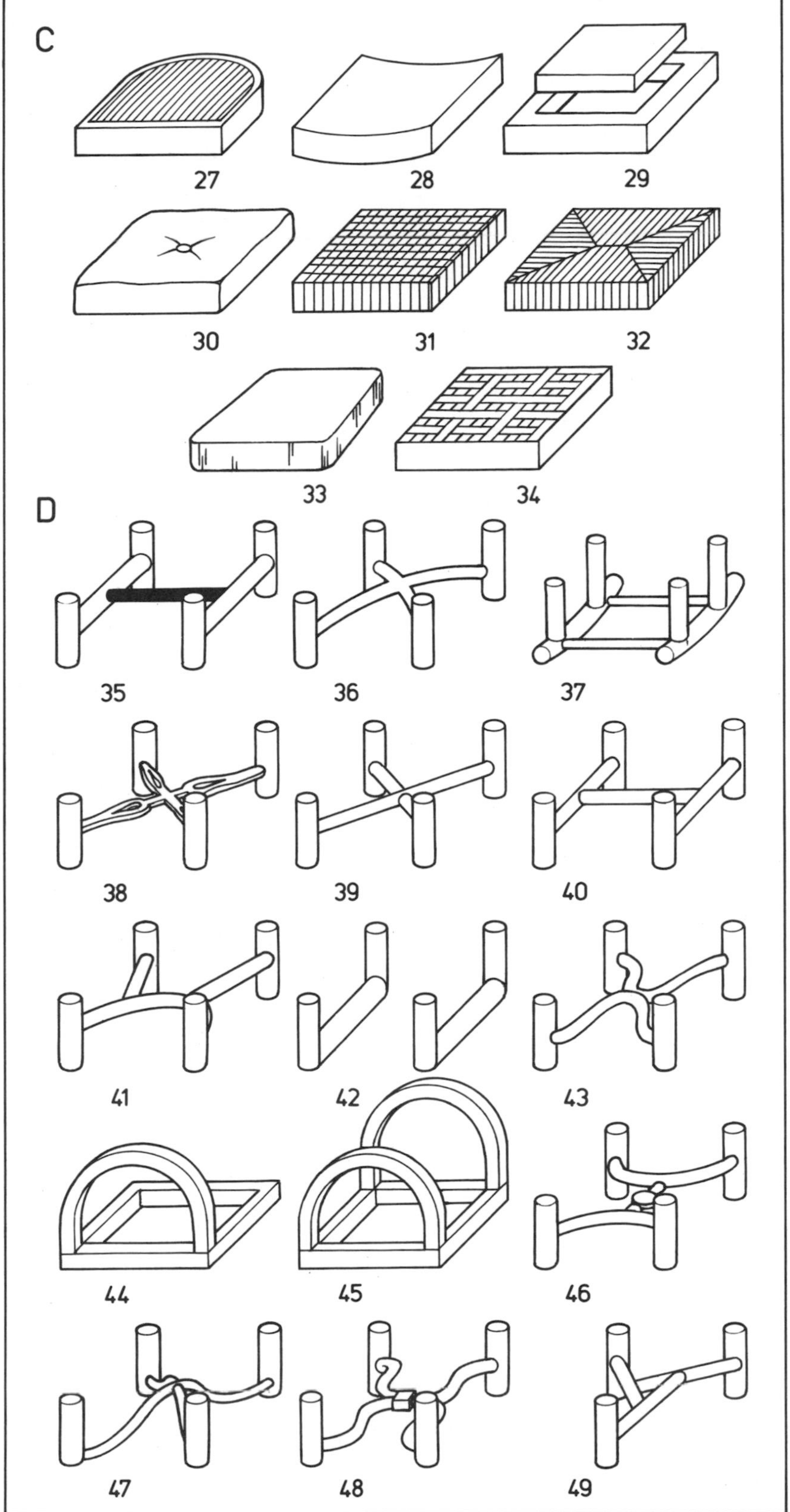

2.04

CONSTRUCTION AND PARTS
DESK AND CABINET CONSTRUCTION

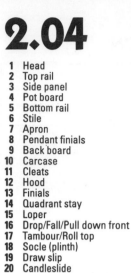

1 Head
2 Top rail
3 Side panel
4 Pot board
5 Bottom rail
6 Stile
7 Apron
8 Pendant finials
9 Back board
10 Carcase
11 Cleats
12 Hood
13 Finials
14 Quadrant stay
15 Loper
16 Drop/Fall/Pull down front
17 Tambour/Roll top
18 Socle (plinth)
19 Draw slip
20 Candleslide
21 Pigeonholes and secret drawer catch
22 Secret drawer
23 Sash door
24 Sight size
25 Glazing bead
26 Glazing bars
27 Lug support
28 Corbel

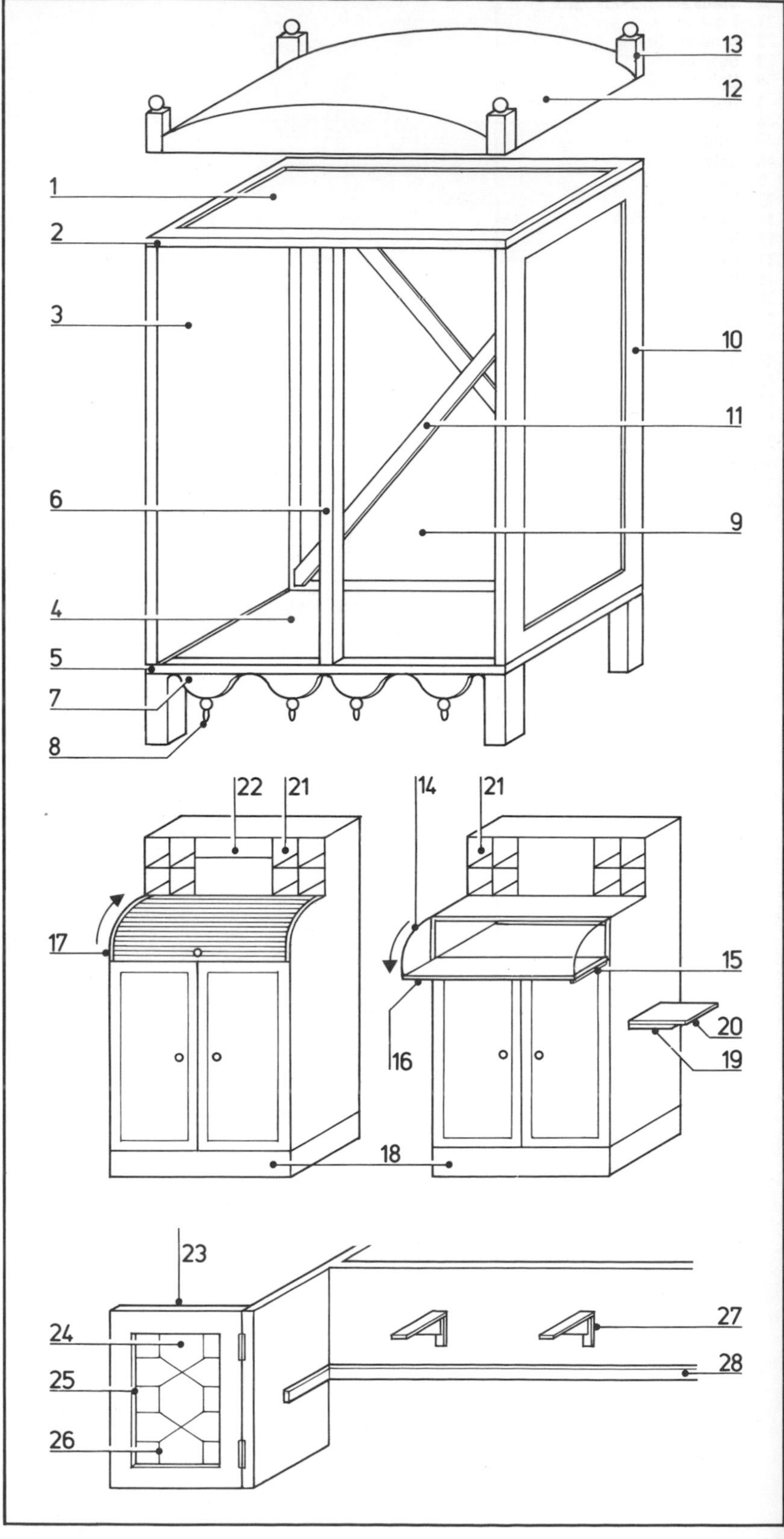

2.05

CHEST AND DRAWER CONSTRUCTION

A Chest and drawer parts
1 Top rail
2 Drawer runner
3 Bearing rail
4 Dust board
5 Bottom rail
6 Leg
7 Post
8 Side panel
9 Side rail
10 Top
11 Drawer front
12 Handle
13 Drawer bottom
14 Drawer back
15 Drawer side
16 Quadrant drawer

B Brackets
17 Bracket
18 Pierced
19 Clock
20 Console

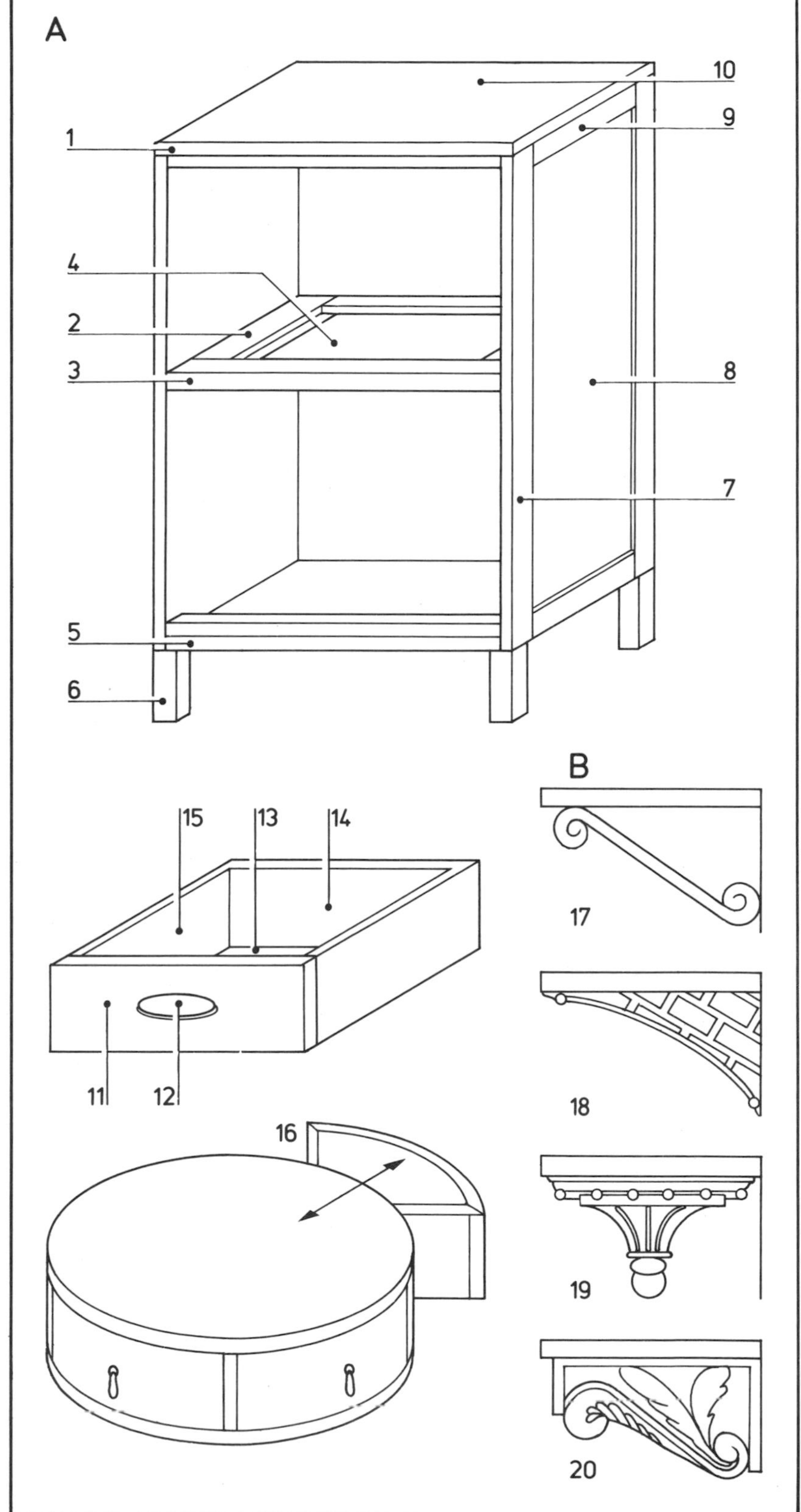

2.06

CONSTRUCTION AND PARTS
TABLE CONSTRUCTION

A Parts
1 Gallery
2 Table top
3 Frieze rail
4 Skirting
5 Leg
6 Stretcher
7 Truss

B Table tops
8 Fold over/Concertina
9 Draw leaf
10 Drop leaf
11 Extended

C Sliding panels
12 Slider
13 Fly rails
14 Swords

D Types of support
15 Pedestal
16 Birdcage pedestal
17 Pilasters
18 Legs and stretchers
19 Rudder
20 Gateleg
21 Double gateleg

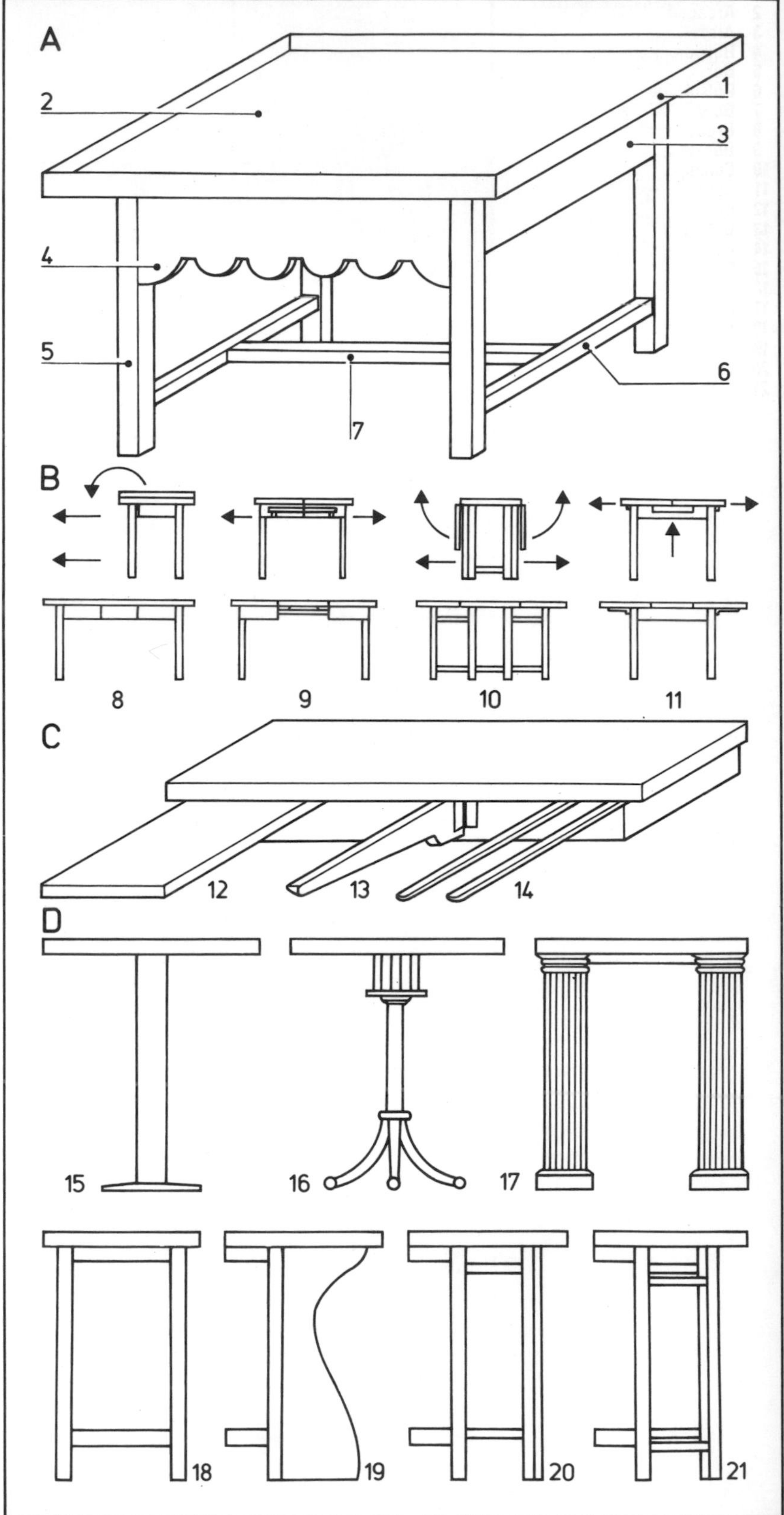

2.07

CONSTRUCTION AND PARTS
CHAIR BACKS 1

1 Anthemion
2 Arcaded
3 Arrow
4 Balloon
5 Bar
6 Bolster top
7 Bow
8 Brace
9 Buckle
10 Camel
11 Cane
12 Comb
13 Crest rail
14 Escutcheon/Cartouche
15 Fan
16 Festoon
17 Fiddle
18 Gothic scroll
19 Hoop
20 Ladder
21 Lath

2.08

CONSTRUCTION AND PARTS
CHAIR BACKS 2

22 Lyre
23 Open padded
24 Pierced splat
25 Pillow top
26 Prince of Wales feathers
27 Rope
28 Rope and rail
29 Scroll
30 Shawl
31 Sheaf
32 Shield
33 Shield and feathers
34 Slat
35 Spindle
36 Splat
37 Square
38 Tablet
39 Three back
40 Wavy slat
41 Wheel
42 X-frame

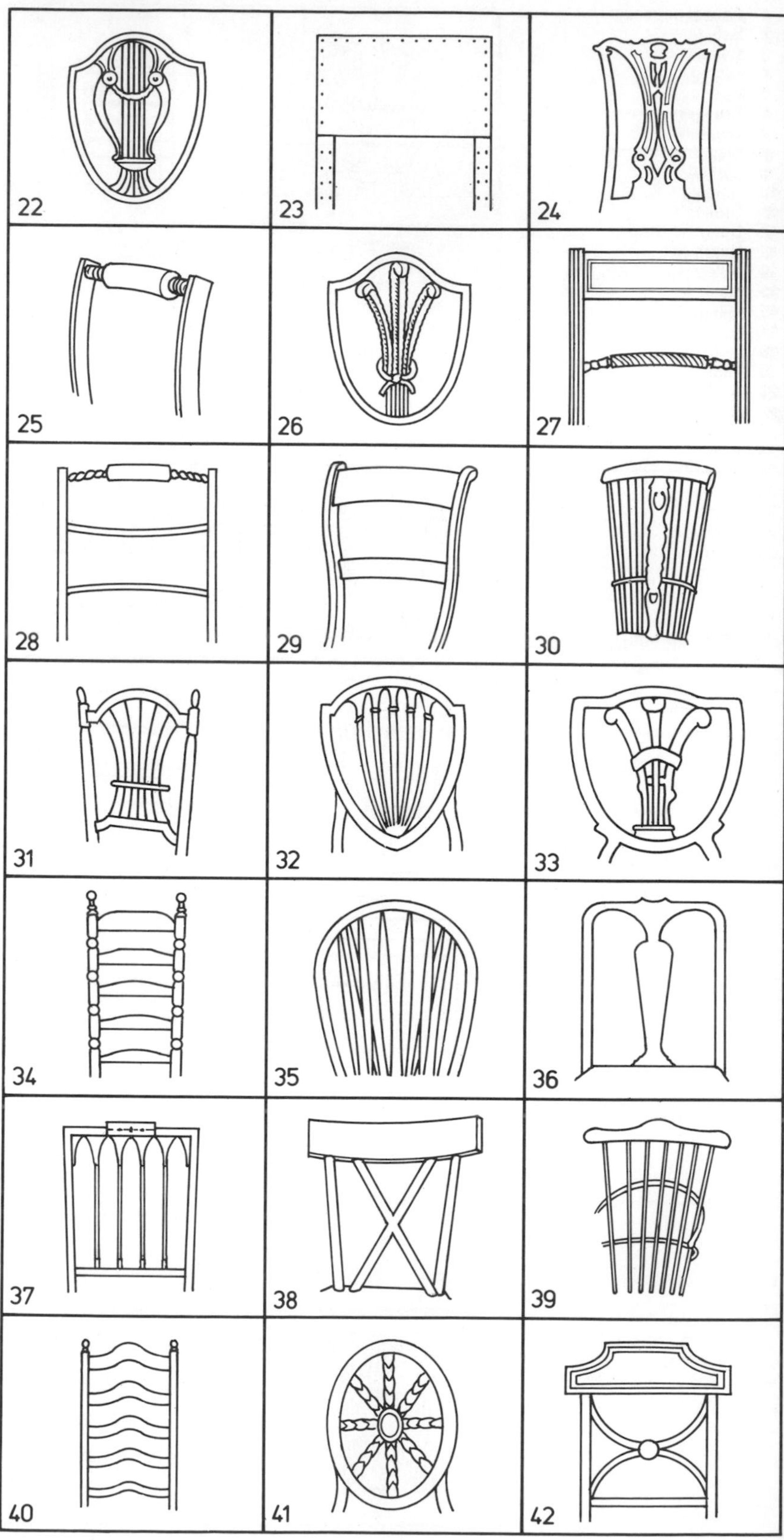

2.09

CONSTRUCTION AND PARTS
FEET

1 Animal couchant
2 Ball
3 Ball and claw
4 Block
5 Bootjack
6 Bracket
7 Bun (onion)
8 Claw (rat)
9 Cloven
10 Dolphin
11 Drake
12 Dutch (US)/Pad
13 Dutch angular
14 Dutch groved
15 Flemish scroll
16 Flemish bracket
17 Gutta
18 Hoof
19 Leaf scroll
20 Melon
21 Ogee
22 Paw (dog)
23 Pear
24 Sabot
25 Scroll
26 Shell
27 Spade
28 Spanish/Braganza
29 Splay
30 Stub
31 Tern
32 Turnip

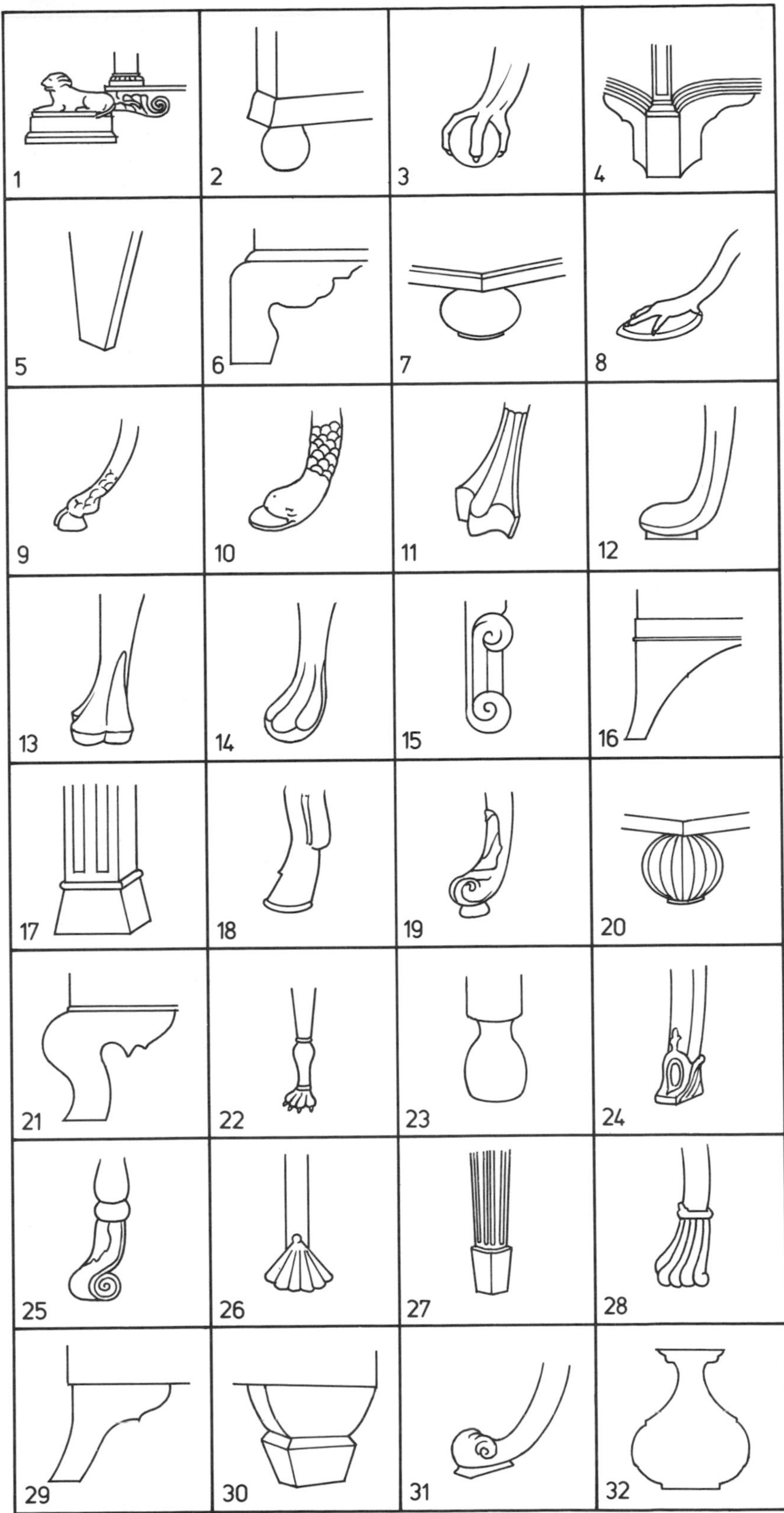

2.10

CONSTRUCTION AND PARTS
LEGS

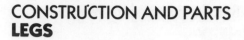

1 Ball turned
2 Baluster
3 Bobbin turned
4 Bulbous
5 Cabriole
6 Cluster column
7 Columnar
8 Cupped
9 Elephant trunk
10 Flemish scroll
11 Fluted and square tapered
12 Fretted
13 Hock
14 Marlborough
15 Melon-bulb
16 Reeded
17 Sabre
18 Scroll
19 Scroll top
20 Spiral
21 Straight moulded
22 Stump
23 Tapered and turned
24 Trumpet
25 Turned and fluted

2.11

CONSTRUCTION AND PARTS
TURNERY

1 Acorn
2 Ball
3 Ball and reel
4 Baluster
5 Bamboo
6 Bead and ball
7 Bell and baluster
8 Block and vase
9 Bobbin
10 Bulb
11 Bulbous
12 Bun foot
13 Columnar
14 Cup
15 Cup and cover
16 Double twist
17 Melon bulb
18 Open twist
19 Reel and bead
20 Ring
21 Sausage
22 Spindle
23 Spool
24 Trumpet
25 Turned and fluted
26 Twist
27 Vase
28 Vase and ball
29 Vase, ring and bulb

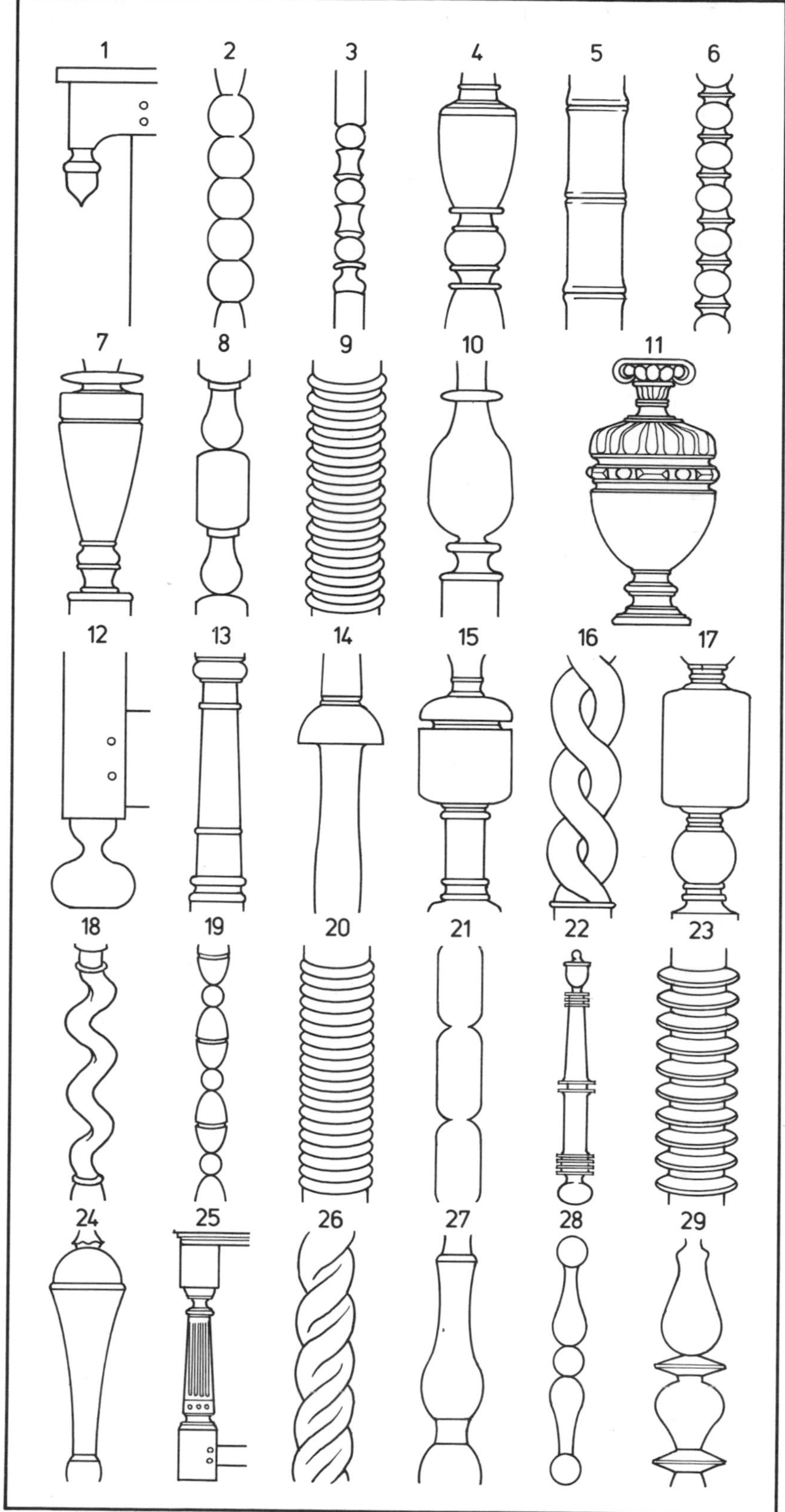

2.12

CONSTRUCTION AND PARTS
HINGES

1 Back flap
2 Butterfly
3 Butt
4 Card table
5 Card table strap
6 Cock's head
7 Hasp (lock-hinge)
8 H-hinge
9 HL-hinge
10 Horseshoe and strap
11 Knobbed butt
12 L-hinge
13 Loop
14 Piano
15 Pin
16 Quadrant (rule)
17 Rat tail (Devil's tail)
18 Rising butt
19 Strap
20 Table rule joint
21 Wardrobe door

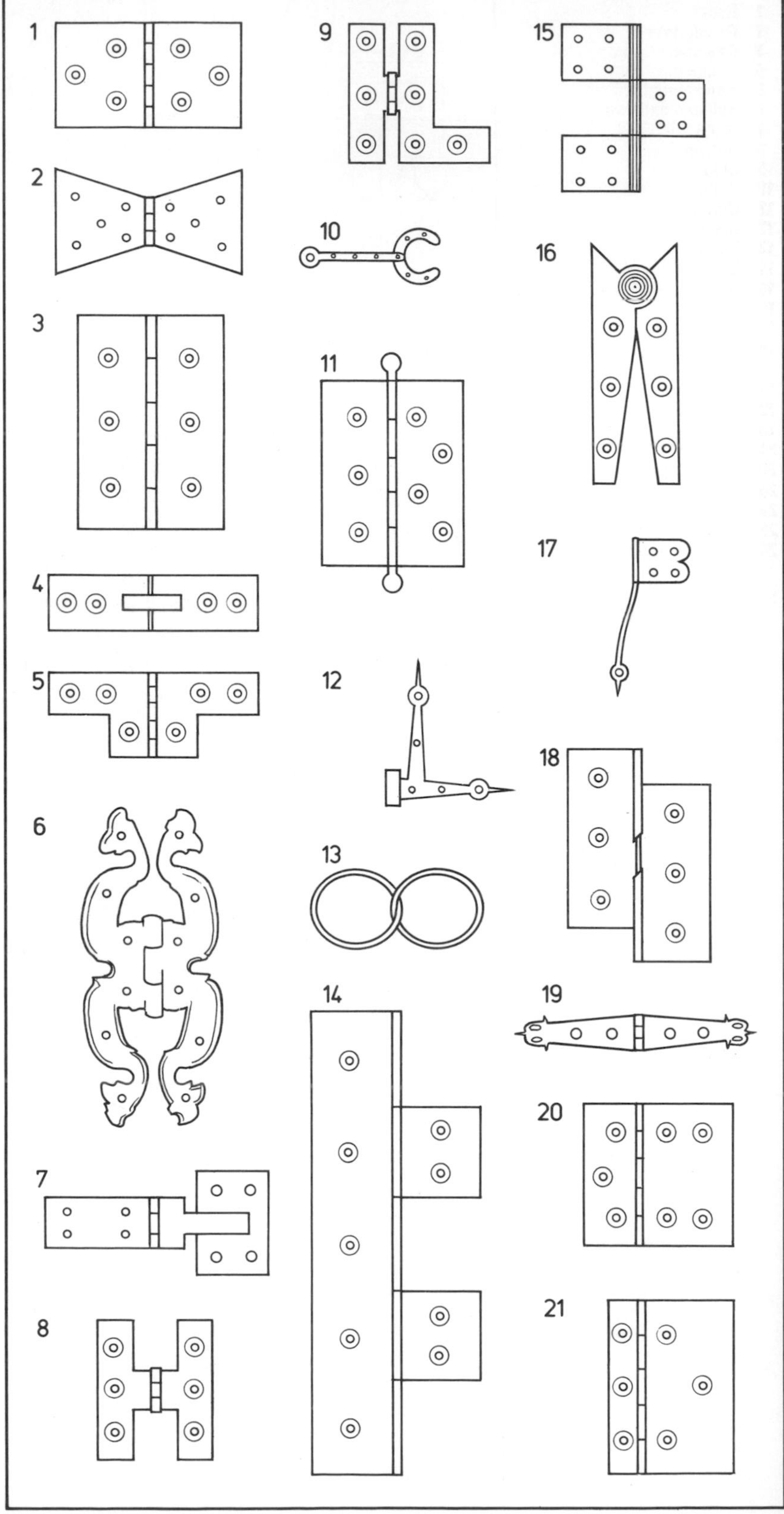

2.13 CONSTRUCTION AND PARTS
HANDLES AND ESCUTCHEONS

A Handles/Knobs
1 Drop
2 Acorn drop
3 Axe drop
4 Pear shape drop
5 Baluster drop
6 Split tail drop
7 Queen Anne drop
8 Stirrup
9 Swan neck
10 Plain curved
11 Oval
12 Squared
13 Plain ring
14 Loop
15 Shield
16 Reeded cup
17 Knob
18 Sunk

B Escutcheons/Backplates
19 Solid
20 Pierced
21 Stamped
22 Octagonal
23 Oval
24 Oval and patera
25 Round
26 Lion
27 Campaign (countersunk)
28 Cut away
29 Pivoted keyhole escutcheon

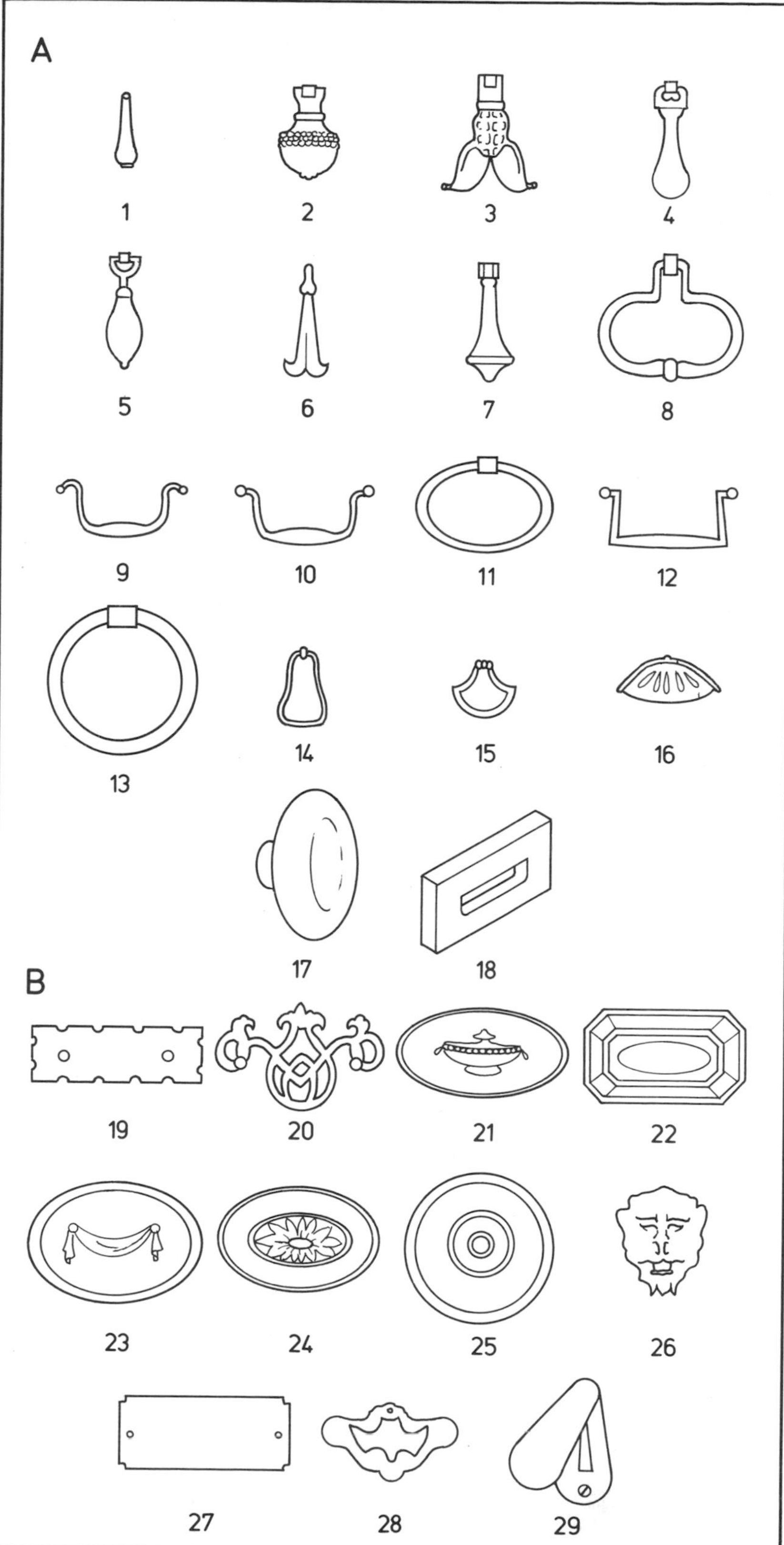

2.14 CONSTRUCTION AND PARTS
PILLARS AND PEDIMENTS

A Pillar parts
1 Cornice
2 Frieze (Flat)
3 Architrave
4 Entablature
5 Abacus
6 Capital
7 Shaft
8 Base
9 Column
10 Pedestal
11 Pediment
12 Finial
13 Pulvinated frieze
14 Volute

B Pediments
15 Flat cornice
16 Cavetto
17 Swell (Pulvinated)
18 Dentil
19 Arched
20 Double arched
21 Treble arched
22 Triangular (gable)
23 Broken arched
24 Broken triangular (gable)
25 Domed
26 Double domed
27 Scroll
28 Lattice (fretted)
29 Swan's neck/Goose neck
30 Swan neck bonnet top
31 Banner top
32 Bonnet top

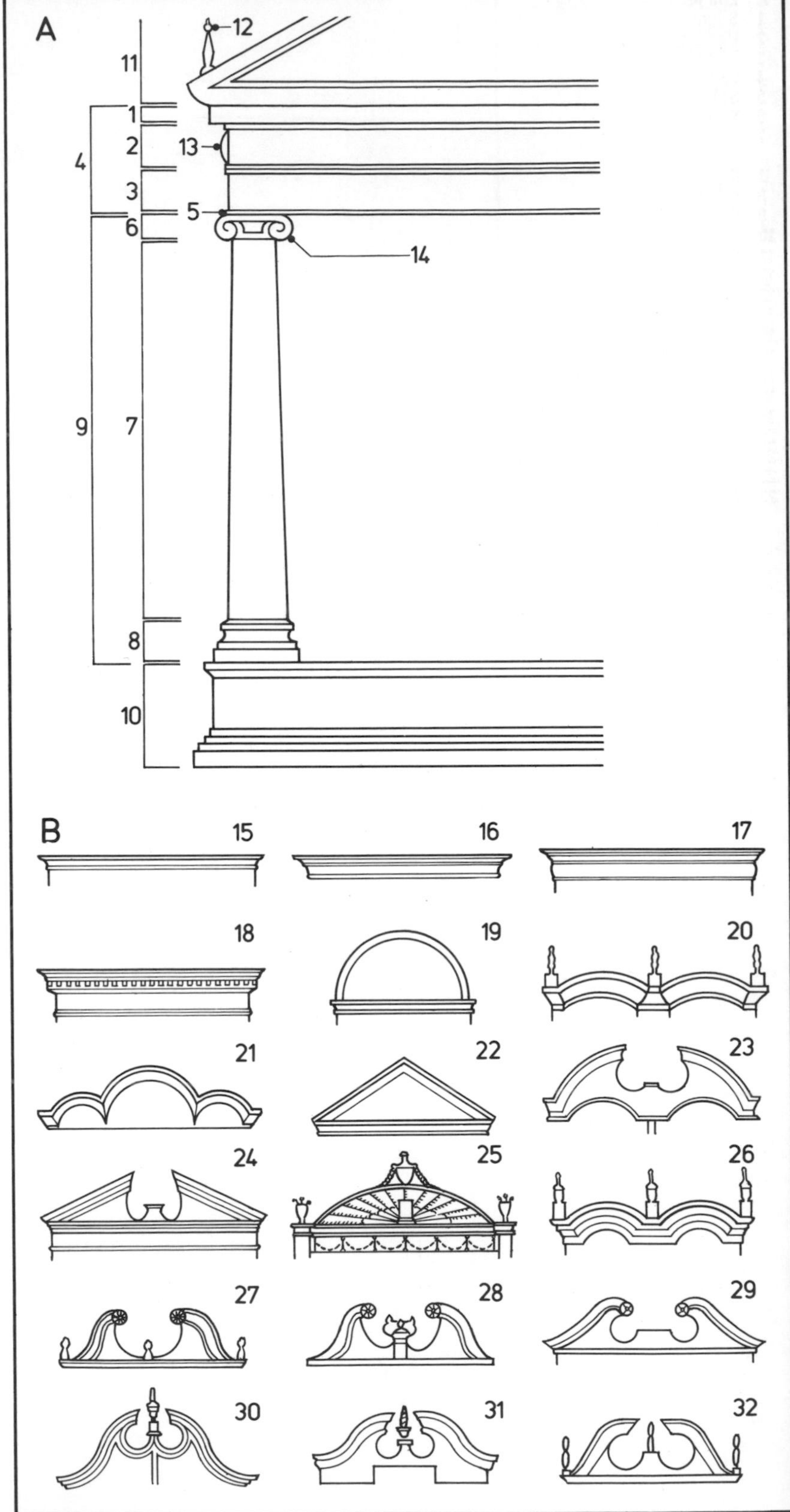

2.15

JOINERY 1

A End joints
1 Squared splice
2 Half lap
3 Finger
4 Lap
5 Splice
6 Scarf
7 Tongued tenon

B Right angled joints
8 Middle lap
9 Cross lap
10 End lap
11 Mitred half lap
12 Plain mitred
13 Quirk mitred
14 Mitred wood spline
15 Ron mitred
16 Ring mitred
17 Dowel right angle
18 Tongue and groove mitre
19 Shoulder mitre
20 Mitred rebate
21 Butt right angle
22 Mitred tenon
23 Two tongued mitre

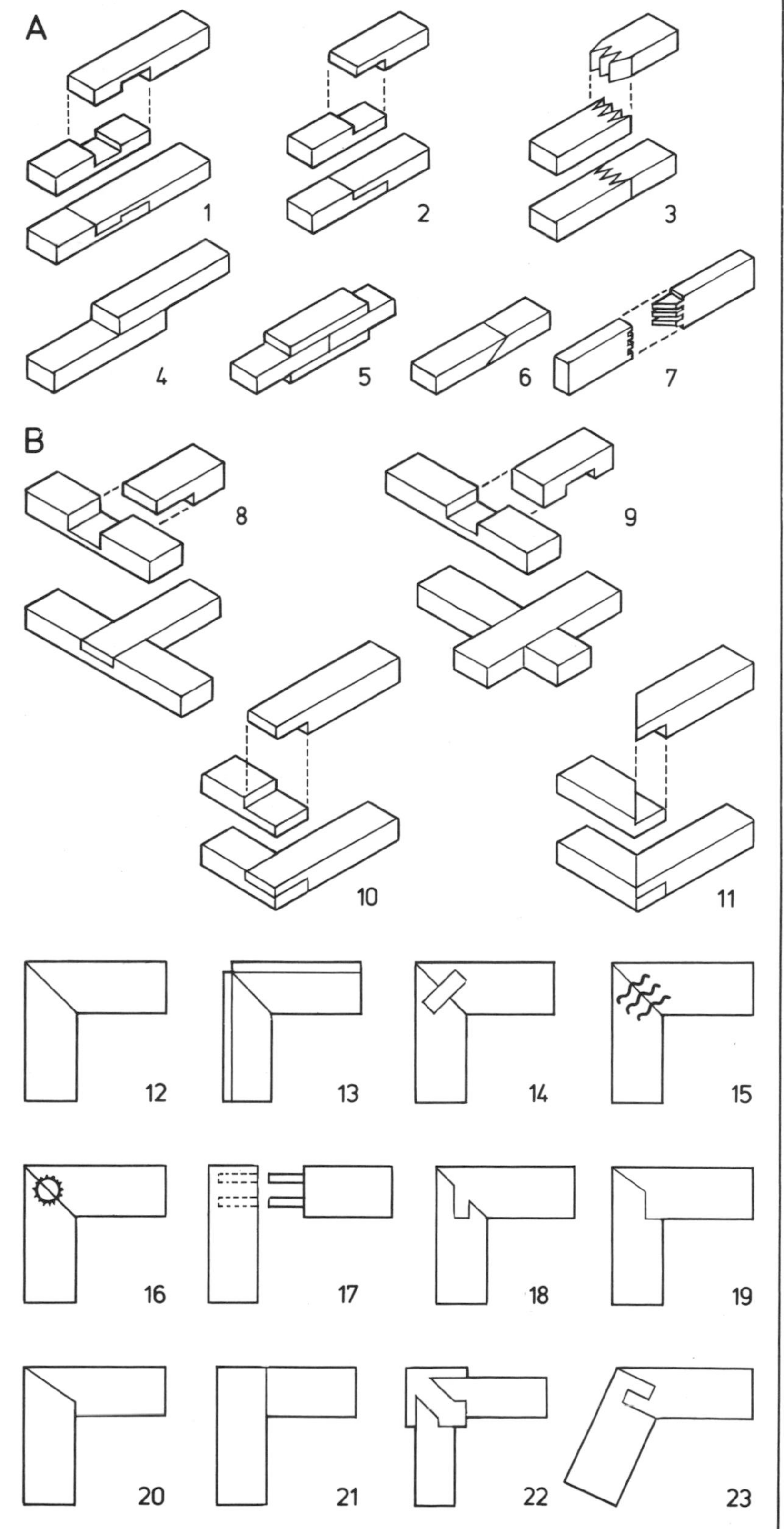

2.16

CONSTRUCTION AND PARTS
JOINERY 2

C Edge joints
24 Butt
25 Ship lap
26 Butterfly
27 Tongue and groove
28 Dowel
29 Fillet
30 Batten
31 Back batten
32 Spline
33 Butterfly spline

D Corner joints
34 Drawer lock
35 French dovetail
36 Millwork
37 Quarter column
38 Round corner (tongued)
39 Hollow external
40 Canted

E Dado and rabbeted joints
41 Dado
42 Stopped dado
43 Dovetail dado
44 Rabbet
45 Dado and rabbet
46 Dado tongue

F Shelf joints
47 Blind dado
48 Through dado
49 Stop dado

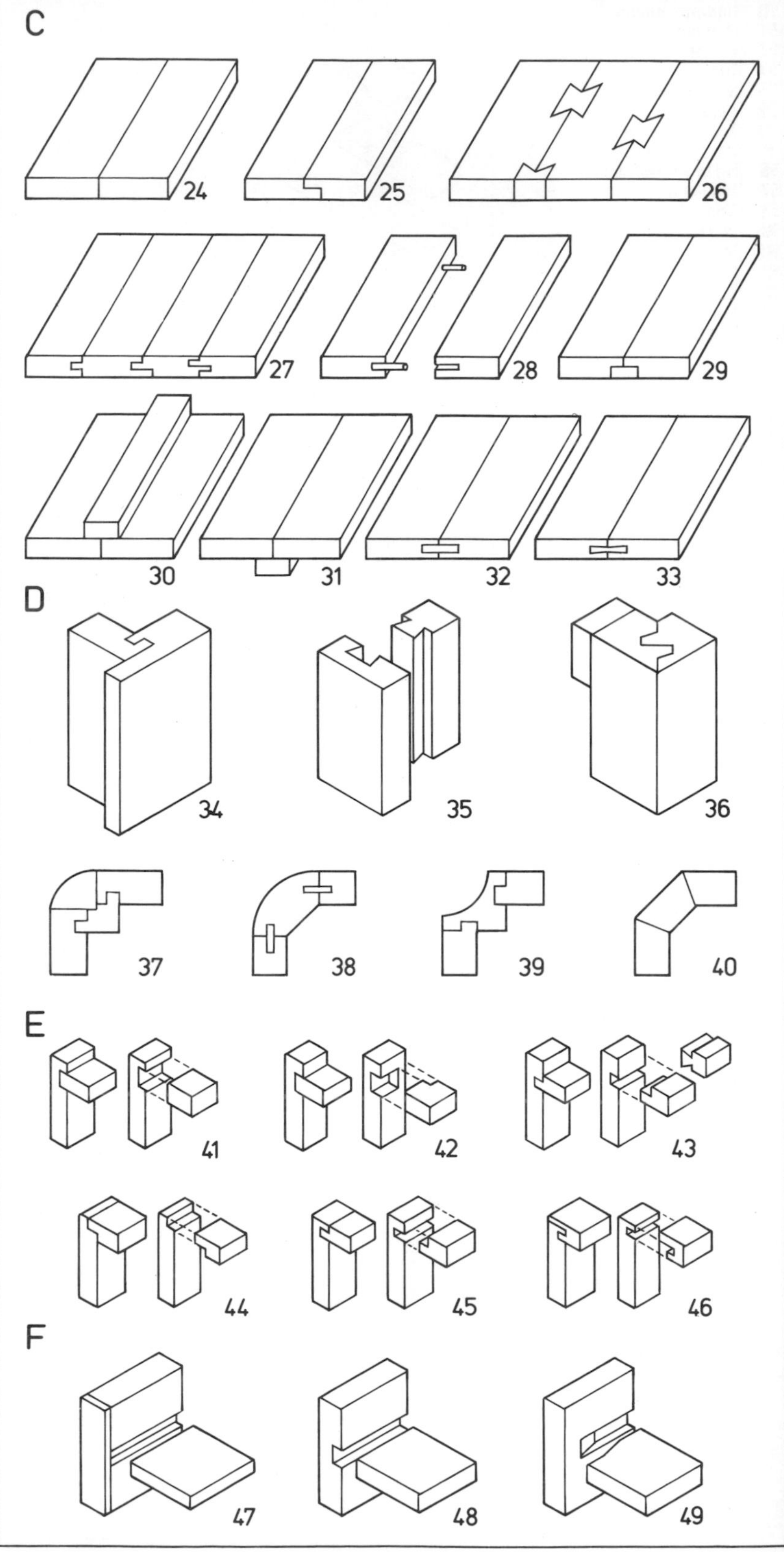

2.17

CONSTRUCTION AND PARTS
JOINERY 3

G Dovetail joints
50 Through single
51 Through multiple
52 Stopped lap
53 Half lap
54 Lap or half blind
55 Blind mitred

H Mortise and tenon
56 Full or Through
57 Blind and stub
58 Wedged
59 Keyed
60 Ship or open
61 Haunch
62 Half blind
63 Haunch blind
64 Pinned blind

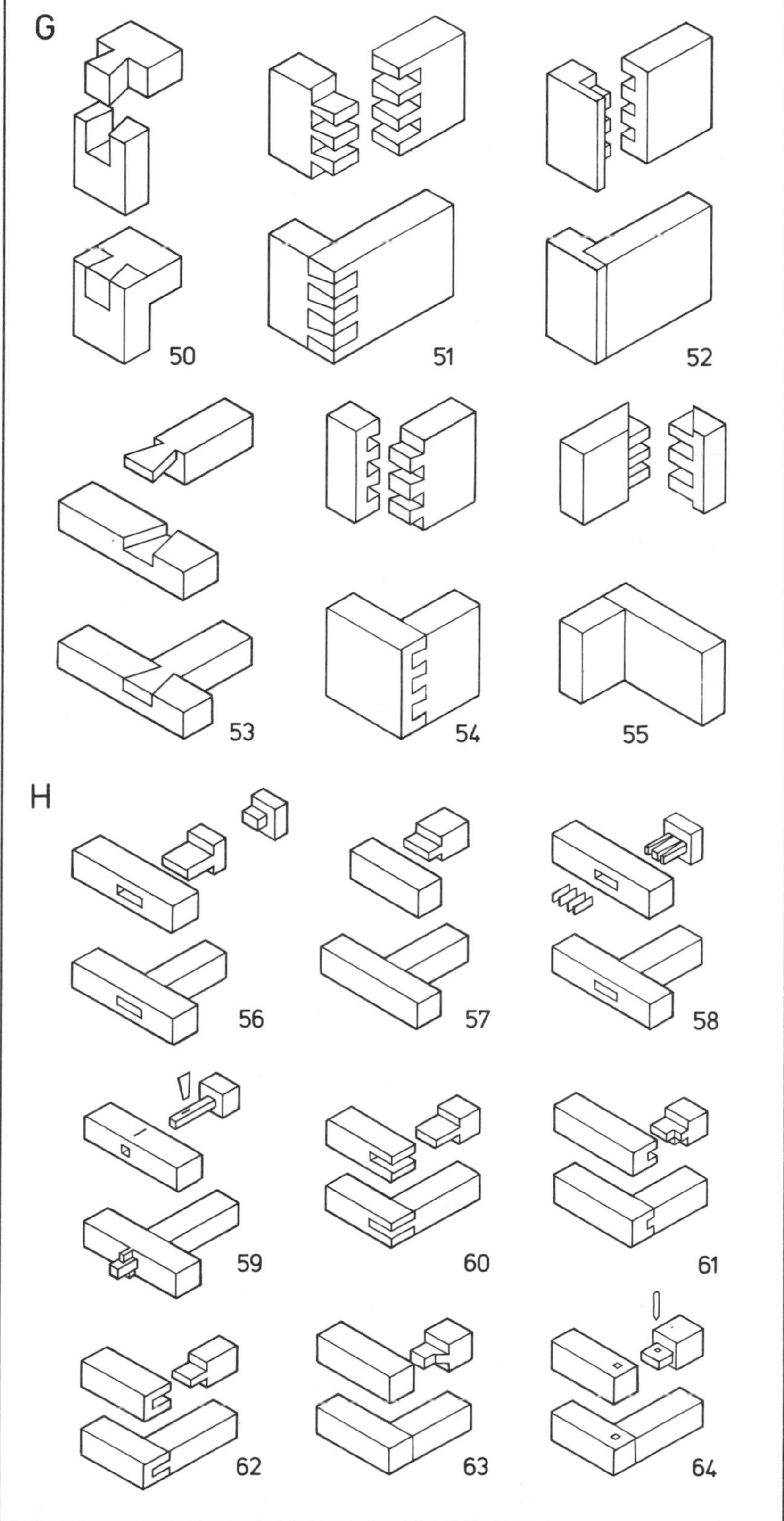

3.01

DECORATION AND FINISH
MOTIFS 1

1 Reeding
2 Fluting
3 Linenfold
4 Key
5 Fret
6 Fret
7 Continuous coil spiral
8 Dentil
9 Square billet
10 Round billet
11 Chevron
12 Chevron
13 Zig zag
14 Peardrop
15 Wave
16 Wave
17 Double cone
18 Bead
19 Reel
20 Bead and reel
21 Gadroon
22 Grape
23 Guttae
24 Egg and dart
25 Egg and tongue
26 Nailhead
27 Dog tooth
28 Tablet flower

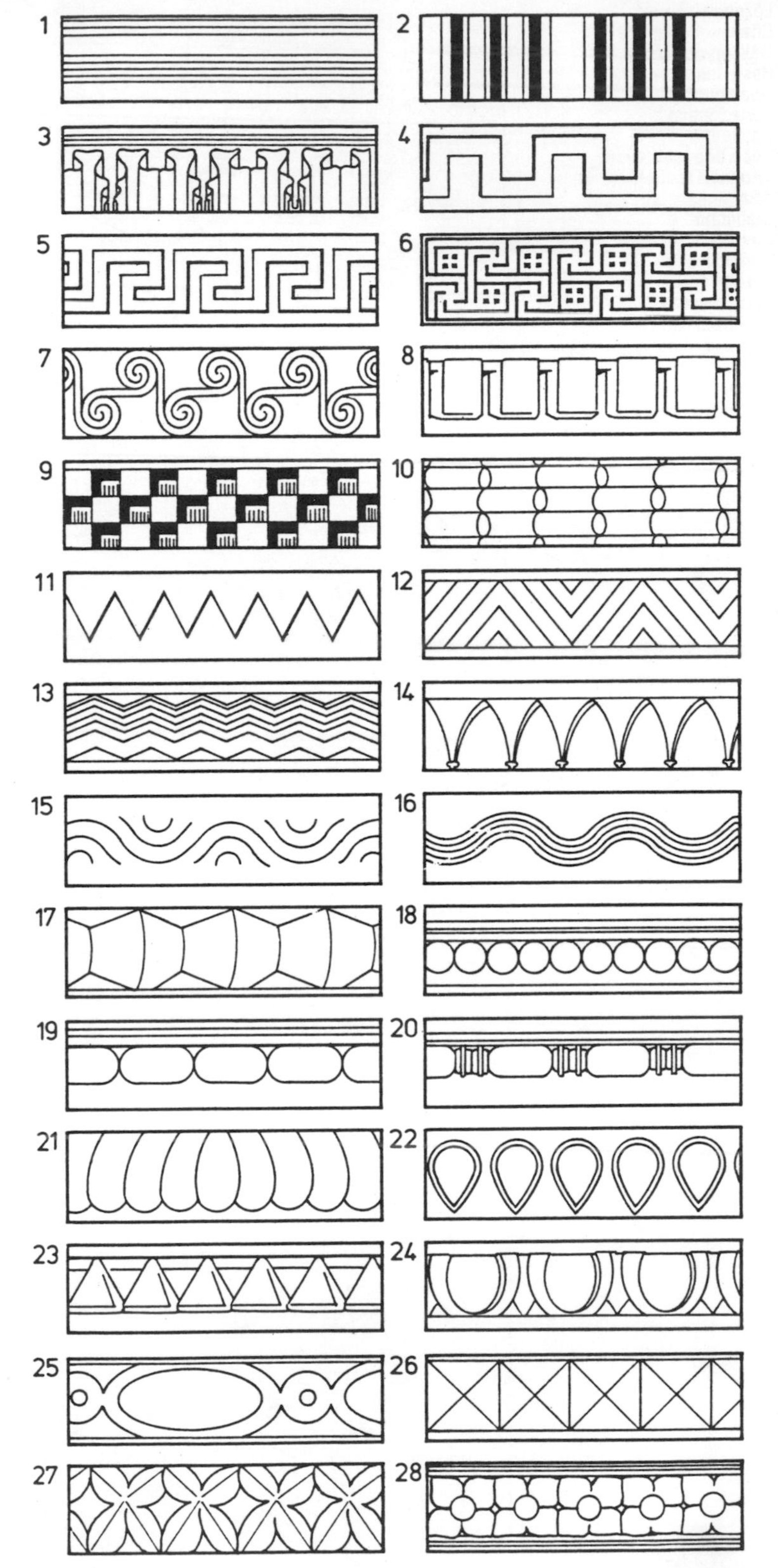

3.02

DECORATION AND FINISH
MOTIFS 2

29 Herringbone
30 Lozenge
31 Chain
32 Ball flower
33 Rose
34 Beakhead
35 Rope (cable)
36 Bay leaf garland
37 Rope and feather
38 Vitruvian scroll/Running dog
39 Guilloche
40 Guilloche
41 Guilloche
42 Scroll (leaf)
43 Scroll/Leaf and rose
44 Vignette
45 Papyrus
46 Festoon
47 Water leaf and tongue
48 Water leaf and dart
49 Lunette
50 Lotus
51 Lotus and papyrus
52 Anthemion
53 Acanthus
54 Anthemion and palmette
55 Anthemion and palmette
56 End scroll

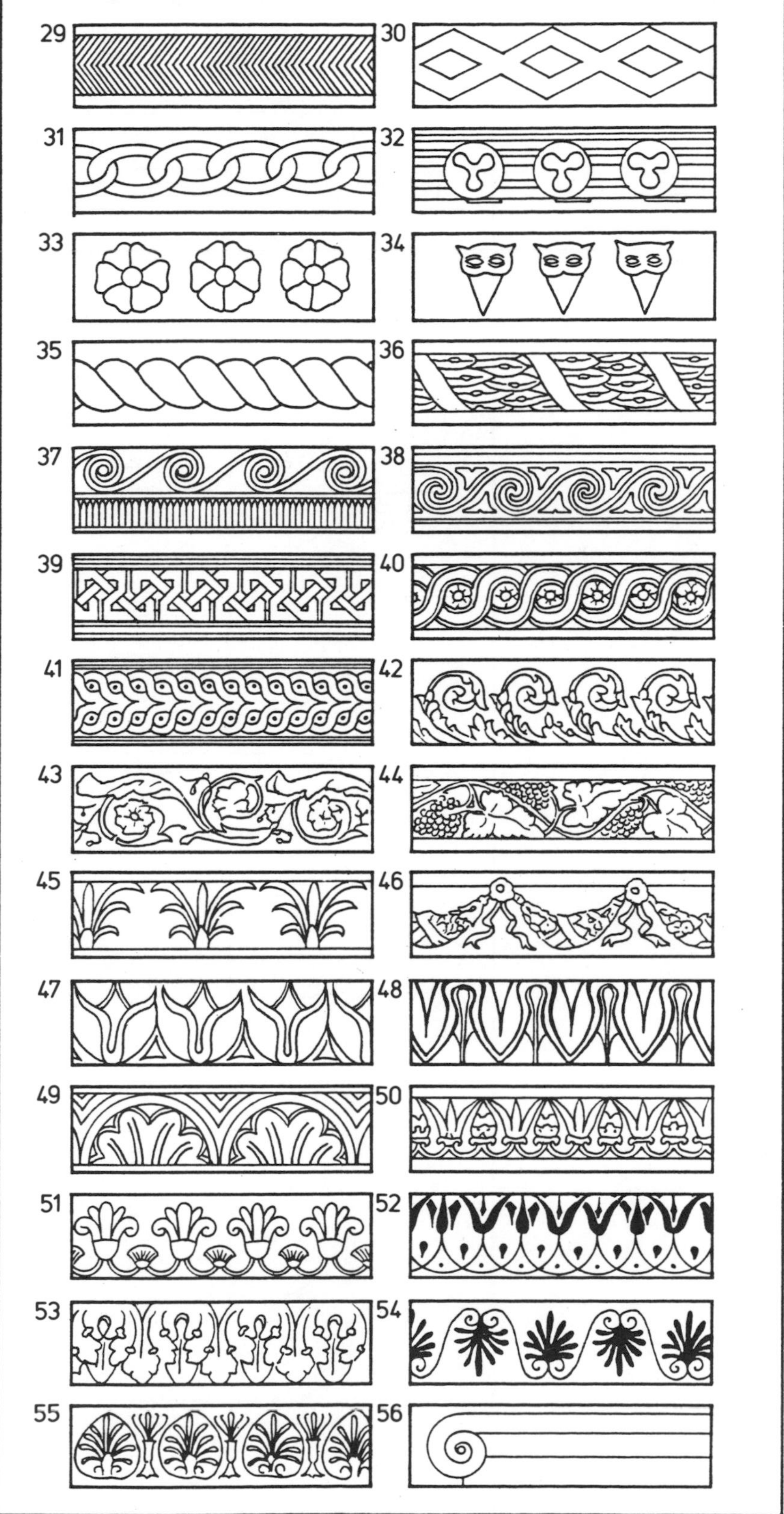

3.03

DECORATION AND FINISH
MOULDINGS 1

1 Fillet raised
2 Fillet sunk
3 Astragal
4 Torus
5 Cavetto (cone)
6 Scotia
7 Hollow
8 Ovolo
9 Round
10 Cyma recta
11 Cyma reversa
12 Beak
13 Thumb
14 Fascia
15 Bevel
16 Quirk
17 Chamfered
18 Thumbnail bead

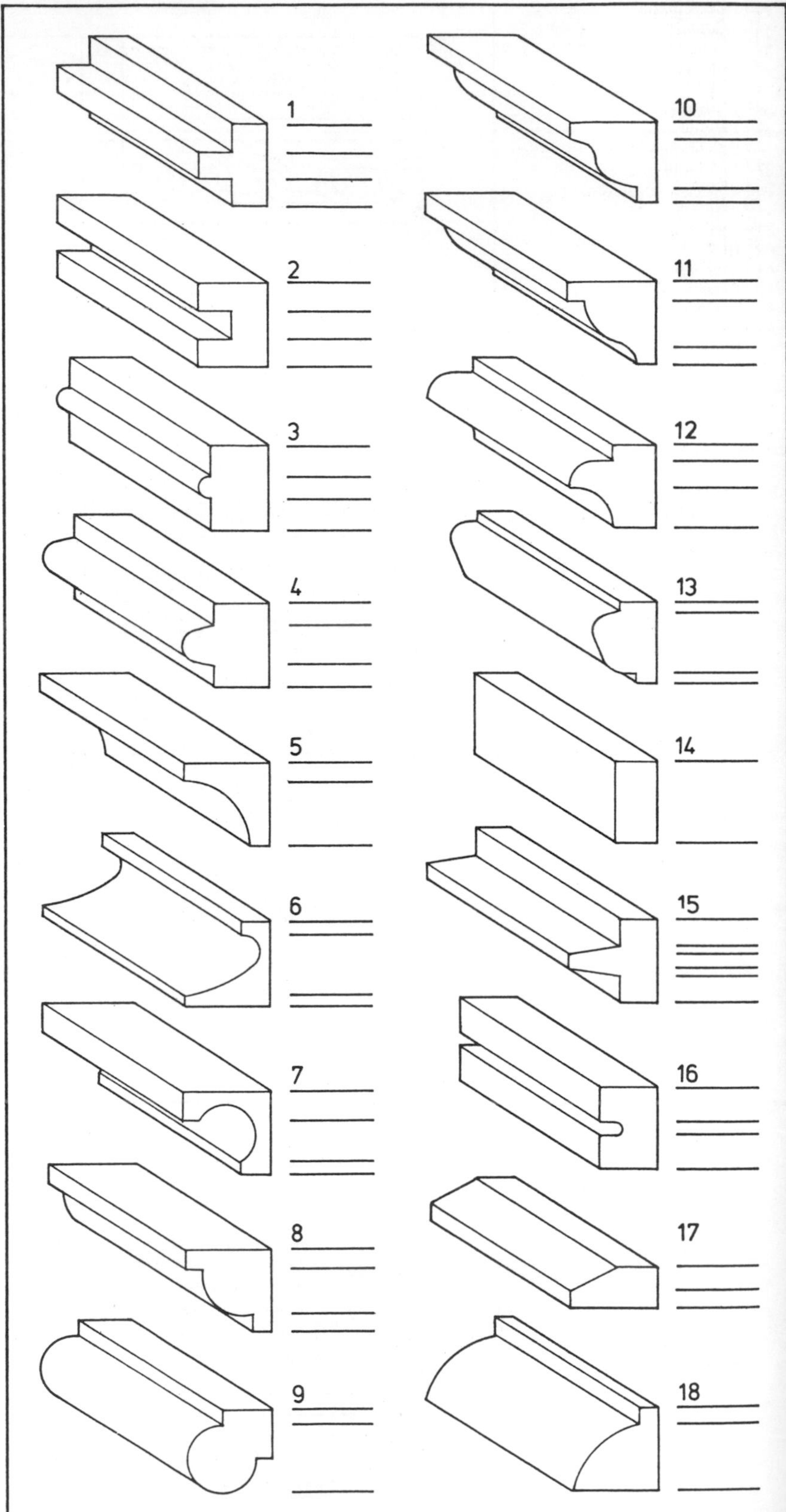

3.04 DECORATION AND FINISH
MOULDINGS 2

19 Cock bead
20 Rope torus
21 Fluted torus
22 Reeded torus
23 Reed and tie
24 Quirk bead
25 Dentil
26 Flush bead
27 Scroll
28 Keel
29 Nailhead
30 Ogee
31 Reverse ogee
32 Corona
33 Billet
34 Bead and reel
35 Beaded

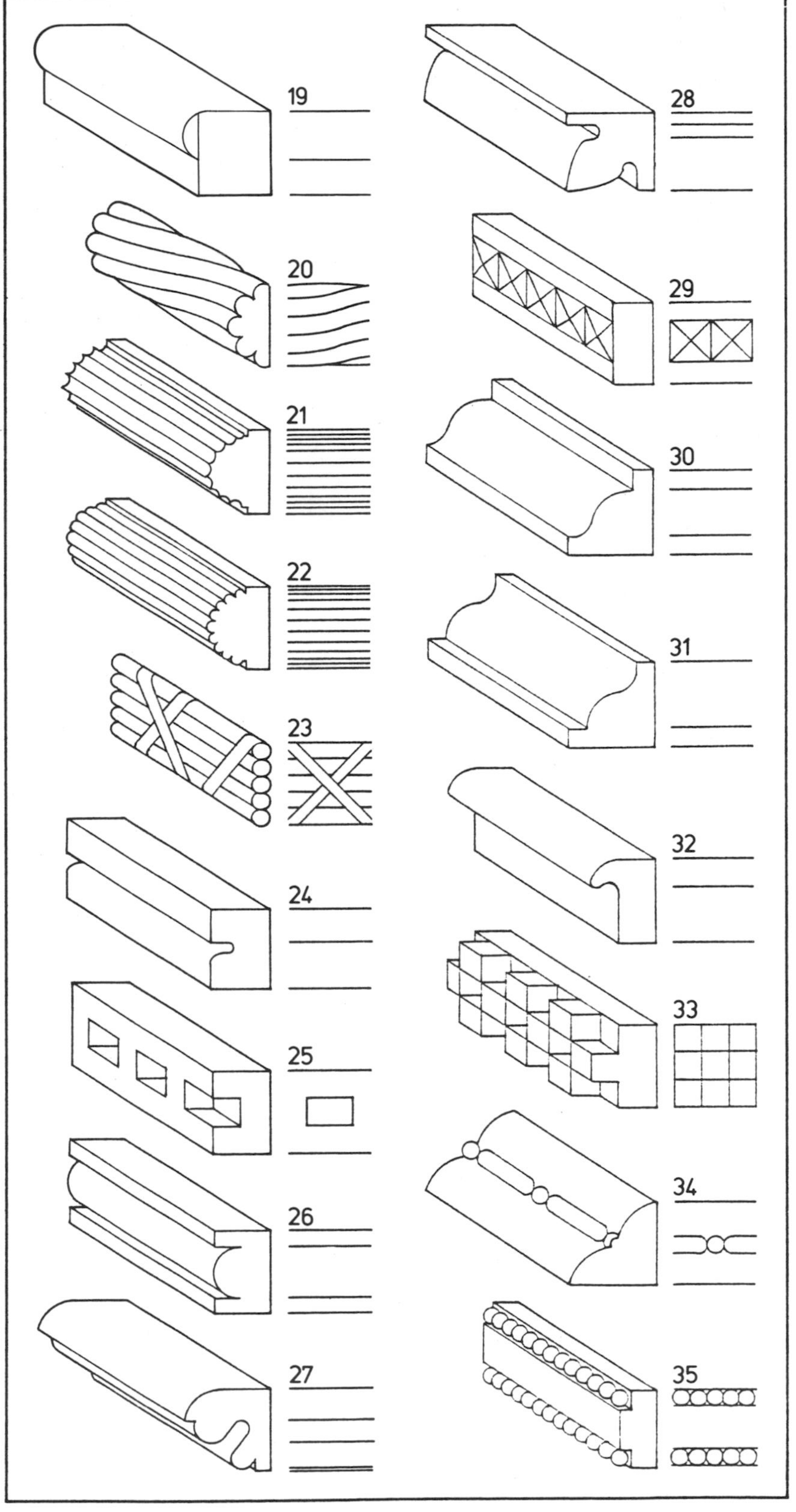

3.05

DECORATION AND FINISH
SHAPE AND FORM

A Form
1 Blockfront
2 Bombe
3 Bowfront
4 Breakfront
5 Demilune
6 Kettle base front
7 Niche
8 Panel
9 Serpentine front
10 Straight front
11 Sweep front
12 Swell front
13 Segmental arch
14 Serpentine top
15 Shell top

B Shape
16 Entasis
17 Tapered
18 Canted
19 Stepped curve
20 Splay
21 Scribing

C Surface
22 Dished corner
23 Countersink and pellet
24 Dishing
25 Sauce edge top
26 Sunk top

D Panelling
27 Arcaded
28 Bead and butt
29 Bead and flush
30 Fielded (raised)
31 Sunk
32 Linenfold
33 Landscape grain
34 Vertical grain

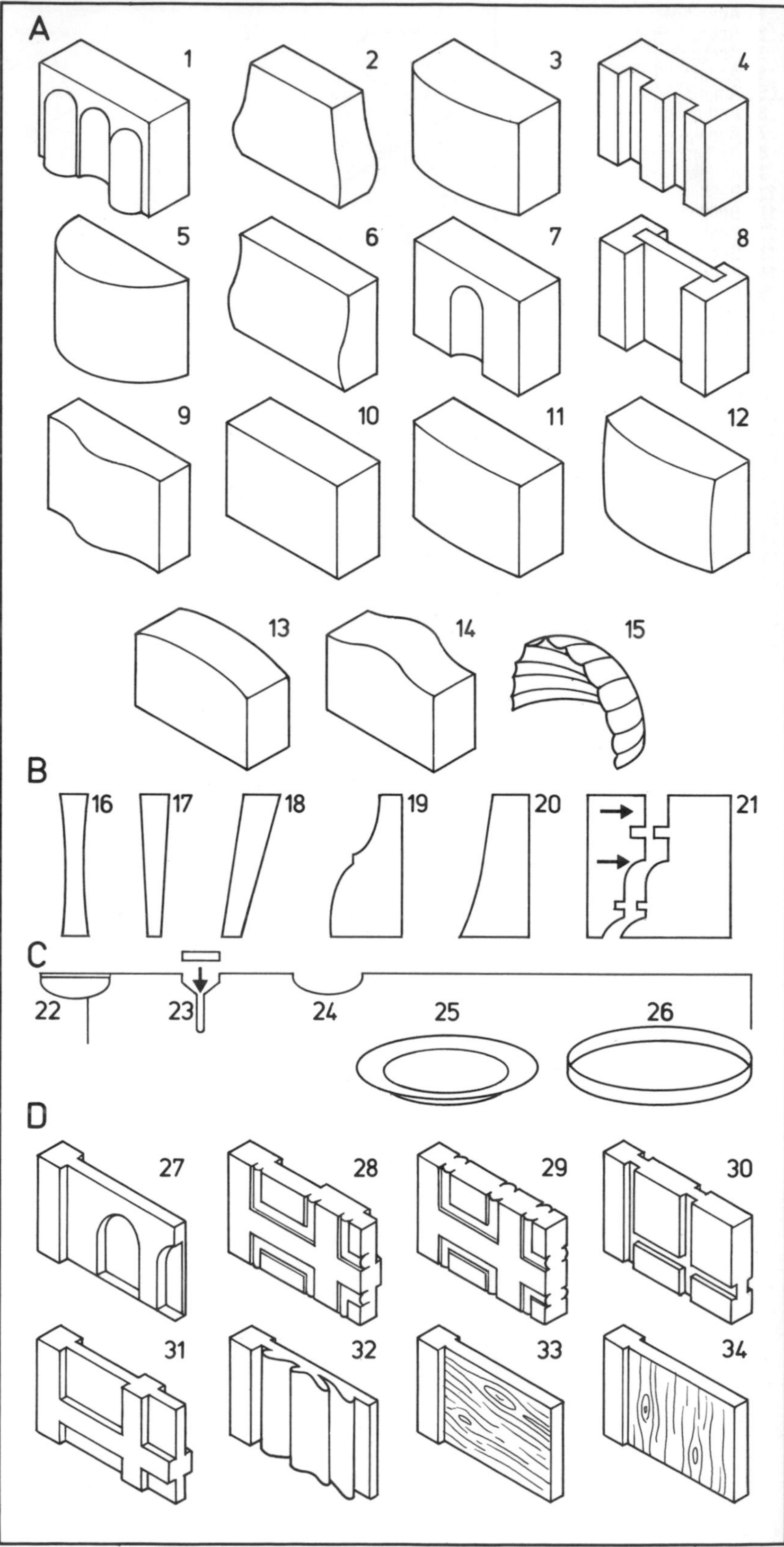

3.06

DECORATION AND FINISH
DEVICES 1

1 Acanthus
2 Acorn
3 Acroterion
4 Amorini (1)
5 Amorini (2)
6 Anthemion (honeysuckle)
7 Appaumé
8 Arabesque
9 Atlanta (female: Caryatid)
10 Bellflower
11 Bellflower brattishing
12 Boar rampant
13 Boar's head couped
14 Cabochon
15 Cartouche
16 Cherub
17 Chimera
18 Chip carving
19 Cockatrice
20 Crocket
21 C-scroll
22 Cyma curve
23 Diamond point (lozenge)
24 Dog rampant
25 Dog's head couped
26 Dolphin
27 Dolphins (two)
28 Dragon
29 Eagle
30 Eagle, two-headed
31 Espagnolette
32 Fan

3.07

DECORATION AND FINISH
DEVICES 2

33 Fan (quarter)
34 Fish hauriant
35 Fretwork
36 Garb
37 Gouge carving
38 Griffin
39 Grotesque sphinx
40 Hawk
41 Horse rampant
42 Imbrication
43 Initials
44 Kylix
45 Laurelling
46 Leopard's face
47 Lion coward
48 Lion (demi-lion)
49 Lion passant
50 Lion passant guardant
51 Lion queue fourchee
52 Lion rampant
53 Lion rampant guardant
54 Lion salient
55 Lion sejant
56 Lion sejant rampant
57 Lion's face
58 Lion's head
59 Lion's paw couped
60 Lion statant
61 Lion statant guardant
62 Lotus
63 Lyre
64 Martlet

3.08

DECORATION AND FINISH
DEVICES 3

65 Mermaid
66 Nulling
67 Patera
68 Pelican
69 Poppyhead
70 Prince of Wales feathers
71 Rosette
72 Sabot
73 Scratch carving
74 Seiren/Siren
75 Serpent nowed
76 Serpent vorant
77 Shell
78 Sphinx
79 Split spindle
80 Stag at gaze
81 Stag's head cabossed
82 Stag trippant
83 Strapwork
84 Sunburst
85 Sunflower (after carving)
86 Swag
87 Swan
88 Tree (fir tree eradicated)
89 Tree (oak tree on mount)
90 Triquetra
91 Vol
92 Wheatshuck
93 Whiplash curve
94 Whorl
95 Wreath
96 Wyvern

Adam: urn and pedestal 1773

Adirondack: rocking chair

American Chippendale: mahogany lowboy, Maryland c1770

American Moderne: dressing table and stool by Paul Frankl 1930

American William and Mary: slant (sloping) front desk c1690

Aalto, Hugo Alvar Henrik [1899–1976]: Finnish architect who also designed much wooden furniture from the 1920s, transferring the new tubular steel cantilever to his laminated bent plywood chairs. Founded Artek of Helsinki (1935) to make and sell his furniture and furnishings.
Abacus (2.14): a flat area at the top of a capital, dividing a column from its entablature.
Abbotsford period/Baronial style/Monastic style: weighty Regency Gothic (Revival) furniture of the 1820s and 1830s originally made for Sir Walter Scott's Abbotsford home (Scotland).
Abura: hardwood from Nigeria, of light brown colour, easy to stain for furniture mouldings.
Acajou: French for mahogany.
Acanthus device (3.02), **motif** (3.06)
Acorn device (3.06), **drop handle** (2.13), **turnery** (2.11)
Acroterion device (3.06)
Adam, Robert [1728–92]: highly influential Scottish neoclassical architect and designer who, with his brothers, perfected the marriage of furniture and interior design. Ornate Adam furniture was made by Chippendale in the 1760s and 1770s. Introduced satinwood, the Etruscan style, and the sideboard flanked by pedestals.
Adirondack furniture: simple American rural wood style produced from the 1890s to the early 1940s. Named after the mountains in New York state.
Aegricanes: ancient Greek goat's or ram's head motif used on neoclassical furniture from the late 18th century.
Afara: hardwood from West Africa, from dark brown to yellow in colour.
African mahogany: hardwood from West Africa used since the late 19th century as a substitute for the dwindling varieties of both Americas, Cuba and Honduras.
African walnut: hardwood from West Africa.
Afrormosia: hardwood from West Africa, similar to teak and has supplanted it since 1945.
Afzelia: hardwood from Africa that looks like mahogany. Usually used for table tops.
Alcove bed (1.01)
Alder: hardwood from America and Europe, the latter more often a plywood constituent.
Almirah: Anglo-Indian word for movable cup.
Amaranth: see Purple heart.
Amboyna/Amboina wood: hardwood from East Asia named after the Moluccan island. Light red to rich brown in colour, used in some ancient Roman furniture and returned to Europe in the 18th century where much favoured by French Rococo and British Regency cabinetmakers.
Ambulante table (1.31)
American Chippendale (see style timechart): plainer and more Palladian version of the late 18th century British domestic style. Used local woods, not just mahogany, and rural versions persisted beyond 1800, see Country Chippendale.
American Empire style (see timechart): early 19th century blending of French Empire and British Regency features in which mahogany was followed by rosewood and black walnut (1820s on). C-H Lannuier and Duncan Phyfe were the outstanding makers.
American Jacobean furniture: predominant 17th century Colonial English form, also known as Pilgrim due to most existing examples, especially oak chests, coming from New England. Rectangular, simply decorated and a few basic types.
American Moderne (see style timechart): loose description of a 1930s US style, derived from Art Deco and International Modern, that often incorporated materials such as Bakelite and chrome.
American Queen Anne style (see timechart):Colonial style that started later and lasted longer than in Britain with more solid rather than veneered walnut being used.
American whitewood: see Tulip poplar.
American William and Mary style (see timechart): longer lasting Colonial version of the British style. Walnut and maple wood, together with new tables, desks and cupboards, began to replace oak pieces in wealthy homes.
Amorini (3.06): see Putto.
Andaman rosewood: see Padauk.
Andiron/Firedog: metal support for logs used in a fireplace, often highly decorated.
Angel bed/Lit à la duchesse (1.01)
Animal-couchant foot (2.09)
Aningeria/Anegré: hardwood from Africa, plain yellow and often used for veneering.
Anodising: a metalwork finish.
Antefix: rooftop corner ornament, such as an animal's head or anthemion, on neoclassical case furniture.
Anthemion and palmette motifs (3.02)
Anthemion back chair (1.05), **chair back** (2.07), **motif** (3.02), **device** (3.06): honeysuckle flower device common in classical design from ancient Greece onwards.
Anthenienne stand (1.29)

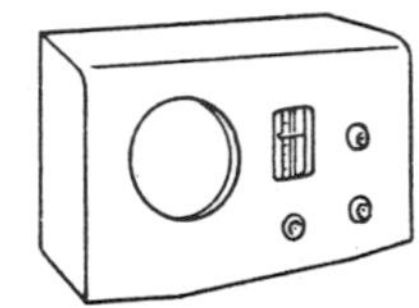
Art Deco: radio cabinet

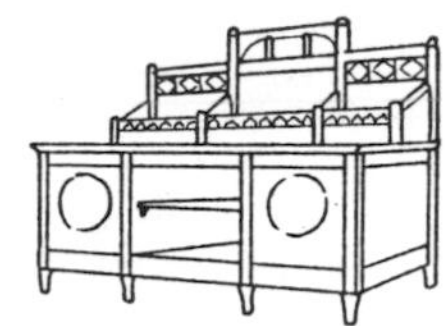
Art Furniture Movement: Modern Gothic walnut sideboard by Bruce Talbert c1867

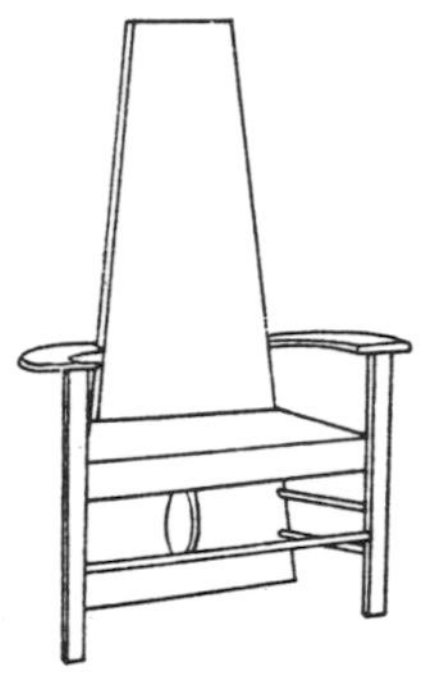
Art Nouveau: armchair

Arts and Crafts Movement: chair by Charles Voysey 1896

Auricular style: Dutch oak armchair early 17th century

Antimacassar: detachable chair/sofa protective cloth against stains from hairdressing macassar oil. By late 19th century mainly decorative although the feature survives in first class railway carriages.
Antique vert: dark green paint on wood to represent the texture of ancient bronze, see Verdigras.
Appaumée device (3.06)
Apple: very polishable, brown-pink hardwood, especially good for turning.
Appliqué/Applied work: ornament or detail made before being attached to furniture. A 16th century Spanish feature that came to England via the Low Countries.
Apron (2.04): bottom frame of a piece of furniture, often carved and ornamented in profile.
Arabesque (3.06): intricate and subtle surface decoration based on a mixture of geometrical patterns, elaborate botanical forms and classical objects.
Arca: treasure chest.
Arcaded chair bak (2.07), **panel** (3.05)
Arch: ornamental feature for furniture.
Arched pediment (2.14), **stretcher** (2.03)
Architect's table (1.31)
Architrave (2.14): in classical architecture the lowest of the three divisions of an entablature.
Ark see Coffer.
Armada chest (1.16)
Armadio cupboard (1.18)
Arm chair (1.05)
Armoire (1.18), **à deux corps cupboards** (1.18)
Arm pad (2.02): part of a chair.
Arm rail (2.02): part of a chair.
Arm stump (2.02): part of a chair.
Arrow (2.02): Renaissance and subsequent classical decorative item.
Arrow back Windsor chair (1.14)
Arrow chair back (2.07)
Art Deco (see style timechart): decorative arts and architectural style emanating from Paris in 1925 and common in both Europe and America. Stylised and modernist, it reconciled methods of mass-production and man-made materials (such as Bakelite) as well as using luxury items. Furniture included metalwork designs.
Art Furniture Movement (see style timechart): British 1860s and 1870s design movement led by Eastlake and Godwin that favoured simplicity but wanted fine design for mass production as well.
Art Nouveau (see style timechart): dominant style of decoration and of avant-garde design in Europe from the 1880s to the Great War. Called Le Modern Style in France, *Jugendstil* in Germany and *Stile Liberty* in Italy. Art Nouveau creatively adapted sinuous natural forms in an attempt to avoid architectural and design styles based on archaeological recreations of the past. Also influenced by Japanese art.
Arts and Crafts Movement (see style timechart): British late 19th century crafts revival inspired by William Morris to return to individual medieval, and thus non-industrial, quality that included deliberately primitive cottage furniture.
Ash: hardwood from many regions. White to pale-yellow, its strength and flexibility make it suitable for framing and bentwood.
Aspen: poplar wood variety most suited to use as veneer.
Assemblage sofa (1.25)
Astragal moulding (3.03)
Atlanta (3.06): carved male figure support, rare in furniture.
Auger flame: corkscrew-shaped finial, often seen on American Chippendale furniture.
Aumbry/Ambry/Almery/Almonry: in furniture, medieval word for food cupboard.
Auricular style (see timechart): Dutch-devised sinuous early 17th century variant on late Mannerist ornamentation. The German description *Knorpelwerk* means 'cartilage work'.
Australian blackwood: hardwood mainly from Tasmania and South Africa.
Avodire : medium wood from Africa, of light yellow colour and widely used for veneer.
Ayous: light, soft wood.
Axe drop handle (2.13)
Bachelor's chest (1.16) Fold-over top extends forward.
Back batten edge joint (2.16)
Back board (2.04): part of a desk or cabinet.
Back flap hinge (2.12)
Backgammon table (1.31)
Backplate (2.13): see Escutcheon:
Backpost (2.02): part of a chair.
Back rest (2.02): part of chair supporting sitter's back.

Back stool (1.05)
Bag table (1.31)
Bahut: French for a small portable medieval luggage chest and now denoting a decorated high cabinet.
Baldacchino: a canopy over an altar, either of fabric and portable, or fixed and supported on columns.
Ball and claw foot (2.09)
Ball and reel turning (2.11)
Ball foot (2.09), **turning** (2.11)
Balloon back (2.07), **chair** (1.05), **Windsor chair** (1.14)
Ball turned leg (2.10)
Baluster (2.02, 2.11): architectural feature used for chair backs, or cupboard cornices, also a type of leg (2.10) for long tables; also the post or pillar supporting the handrail on a staircase. A drop handle (2.13).
Bamboo furniture and turning (2.11): oriental use of bamboo for furniture and interior design, copied in the West since the late 18th century.
Banderole: ribbon ornament, carved or painted, and often inscribed.
Banding: decorative wood pattern inlaid straight, across or in herringbone pattern to contrast with the veneer or the edge of the latter.
Banister: see Baluster.
Banister back chair (1.05)
Bank: long medieval seat.
Banker: (a) a cloth placed over a bank. (b) a rectangular cushion on a banker.
Banner top pediment (2.14)
Banquette stool (1.05), **sofa** (1.25)
Bantam work: 18th century Javanese lacquerwork.
Bar back chair (2.07), **sofa** (1.25)
Baroque (see style timechart): 17th century and early 18th century European furniture of elaborate and ornamental character with a sweeping S-curve to the fore.
Barrel chair (1.05)
Base (2.14): part of a pilaster.
Basket chair (1.05), **stand** (1.29)
Basin stand (1.29)
Bas relief: pattern or decoration carved in low relief.
Basset table/Card table (1.31)
Bassinet bed (1.01), **bath chair** (1.09)
Basswood: see Limewood.
Bast: fibrous flax hemp or inner tree bark for making seats.
Baths (1.39)
Batten edge joint (2.16)
Bauhaus (see style timechart): German school of architecture and design 1919–33. Founded by the architect Walter Gropius, epitomised the marriage of modern design, mass production, industrial design and a Teutonic romantic approach to abstract art. Alfred Arndt (b1898) led the furniture workshop. Housed in Weimar till 1925 and in Dessau until 1932, it was finally closed down by the Nazis and in its diaspora ruled in an austere manner modern architecture and design until the 1970s.
Bay leaf garland motif (3.02)
Bead and ball turning (2.11)
Bead and butt flush panel (3.05)
Bead and reel motif (3.01), **moulding** (3.04)
Bead motif (3.01)
Beaded moulding (3.04)
Beakhead motif (3.02)
Beak moulding (3.03)
Bearing rail: joinery term for any horizontal; load-bearing member.
Beau Brummel dressing table (1.31)
Beds (1.01–1.04): platform for sleeping on.
Bed bolt: in some beds, covered joints bolting the rails to footboard and headboard.
Bed moulding: small moulding on bed's cornice.
Bed post (2.01): pillar at the foot of a bed.
Bedstead: main structural frame of a bed.
Bedstead bolt (2.01): iron nut and bolt joining side rails and bed posts.
Bed steps (1.40): set of two or three low steps giving easier access to a high bed. From late 17th century. In 19th century often combined with a night commode.
Bedstock: Elizabethan-period bedpost standing clear of the bedstead proper.
Beech: commonest European hardwood, dense and light coloured. Lightness makes it suitable for making drawers. Also accepts most kinds of finish. Widely used for 17th to 19th century chairs.

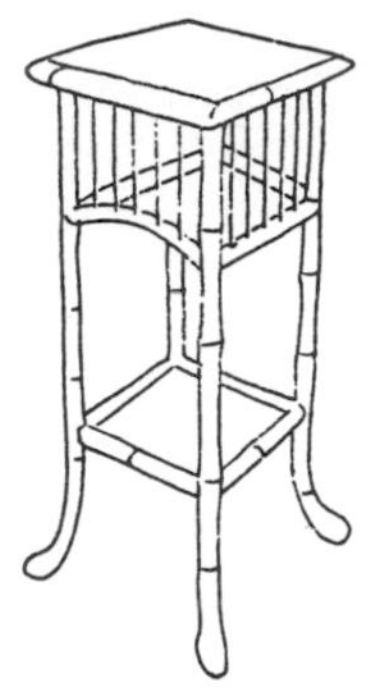
Bamboo furniture: plant stand with tiled top c1900

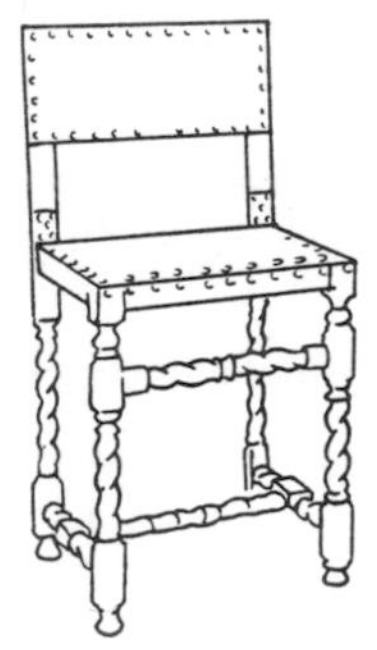
Baroque: leather-upholstered back stool c1650

Belter: Rococo Revival rosewood laminated side chair c1855

Bellflower, Bellflower brattishing (3.06)
Bellini, Mario [b1935]: Italian industrial and office designer whose work includes modular furniture for companies like Cassina. Best known pieces are Chair 932 (1967) and marble/glass Colonnato table (1977).
Belter, John Henry [1804–63]: German, New Yorker from 1844, who made his name synonymous with the New World Rococo Revival. Favoured carving in rosewood and invented a form of bentwood lamination for it together with a mechanical saw.
Bench (1.05, 1.25): long, usually backless seat.
Bent stretcher (2.03)
Bentwood: bending wood into shape by a steam treatment that was used for British 18th century Windsor chairs, but was really established by Thonet (see entry). Breuer and Aalto are 20th century exponents.
Bentwood/Thonet No 14 chair (1.05)
Bérain, Jean [1638–1711]: French Baroque stage and set designer who was Louis XIV's *Dessinateur du roi* from 1674. His furniture designs were imitated across Europe. These lighter, fantastical pieces foreshadowed Regence and Rococo with their chinoiserie, singerie, arabesque and marquetry ornamentation.
Bergère (Chippendale Burjar) **armchair** (1.05)
Bertoia, Harry [1915–78]: American designer active c1937–55 who worked with Saarinen, Eames and Knoll. For the latter he originated mass-produced curved light steel chairs including the classic 1952 Diamond model adjustable to two different angles.
Betty lamp (1.38): 18th century American lamp, either hanging or pedestal.
Bevel moulding (3.03): see Chamfer.
Bible box (1.16)
Bidet: small four-legged stool containing a pan for purposes of personal hygiene. Extant since the late 18th century in portable form.
Biedermeier sofa (1.25) **style** (see timechart): early 19th century simple but homely German interior and furniture design based on French Empire and English Regency neoclassical styles. Popular with the middle class, it spread to Scandinavia and Russia. Furniture came in light coloured woods with ebony ornamentation and horsehair upholstery. Named after a journal's figure of fun. See Danhauser.

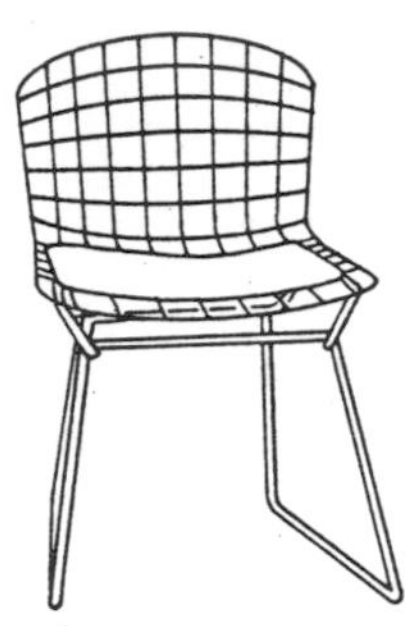
Bertoia: Diamond or Shell wire chair 1952

Bijouterie table (1.31)
Bilboa: 18th century marble-framed mirror from Pacific port of origin.
Billet moulding (3.04)
Billiard table (1.31)
Birch: varied family of pale yellow hardwoods, usually used for cheaper furniture and also Scandinavian Modern designs.
Birdcage/Squirrel cage support/pedestal (2.06): hinged mount on an 18th century tripod table to make it revolve or tilt vertically.
Bird's eye: wood grain veneer effect on maple and other woods, especially popular in America.
Bisellium sofa (1.25)
Black bean: handsome Australian hardwood, usually confined to home-produced furniture.
Blackamoor: Black African male figure used as furniture support in Baroque, Rococo and Victorian styles. Sometimes called a Nubian figure.
Blind joints (2.16, 2.17)
Block and vase turning (2.11)
Block foot (2.09)
Blockfront (3.05): American case furniture front design from c1700 in which two shallow convex section flank a concave centre, particularly associated with Newport, Rhode Island.
Board chest (1.16)
Boar rampant surface decor (3.06)
Boar's head couped (3.06)
Bobbin turned leg (2.10), **turnery** (2.11)
Bodying in: filling a coarse wood's grain before French polishing.
Bog oak: black oak due to immersion in a swamp, occasionally used for Renaissance inlay as ebony substitute.
Bois clair: term given to light woods such as maple, especially for French Restoration style.

Biedermeier style: chair

Bois de bout: see Oyster veneer.
Bois de rose: see Tulipwood.
Bois de Spa: gold chinoiserie on black, a japanning style named after the Belgian health resort which specialised in it.
Bolster arm (2.02), **top chair back** (2.07)
Bombé (3.05), **chest** (1.16): bulging fronts or sides, especially in Louis XV period furniture.

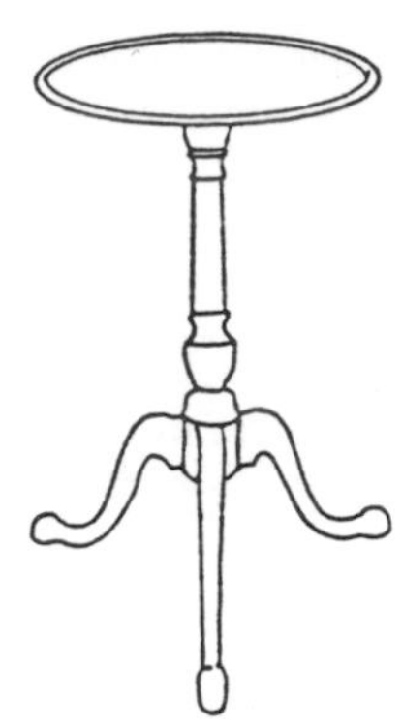
Boston Chippendale: mahogany candlestand 1760-80

Bonheur du jour desk (1.23)
Bonne grâce: bed curtain, 17th century.
Bonnetière cupboard (1.18)
Bonnet top pediment (2.14)
Bookcases (1.18, 1.20, 1.21): unit of bookshelves.
Book stand (1.29)
Bootjack foot (2.09)
Borne sofa (1.25)
Boss: oval or circular ornament often to be found where furniture mouldings intersect.
Boston Chippendale: local American style produced c1755–90 featuring slender cabriole legs, sober ornament and bombé chests.
Boston rocker (1.05)
Bottle end grazing: incorrect term for bullion fringe.
Bottom rail (2.04, 2.05): a structural part of furniture.
Bouillotte table (1.31)
Boulle/Bühl marquetry: elaborate inlay decoration using brass and turtle-shell perfected by Louis XIV's cabinetmaker André Charles Boulle (1642–1732).
Bow back chair back (2.07), **Windsor chair** (1.14)
Bowfront (3.05): convex-curved shape in case furniture.
Bow top (2.02): convex-curved top chair rail.
Box (1.16): see chests.
Box bed (1.01), **settie** (1.25), **stool** (1.05), **stretcher** (2.03)
Boxwood: fine textured pale-yellow hardwood used mainly in the 16th to 18th centuries. Its scarcity reserved it for inlay and small parts.
Brace chair back (2.07)
Bracket (2.05), **foot** (2.09): L-shaped supporting projection from a vertical surface.
Bracing sticks: see Windsor chairs.
Braid: narrow-woven decorative band in upholstered furniture and curtains.
Brass (2.01), **bed** (1.01): metal alloy used as furniture hardware since the 17th century.
Brasses : (a) handles (2.13). (b) keyhole escutcheons (2.13).
Brattishing: Renaissance carved crest at the top of case furniture or screen.
Brazilwood: dark red to orange hardwood from that country, especially adorned early 19th century European furniture.
Breakfast table (1.31)
Breakfront (3.05): furniture with a central section standing out from the two sides.
Breuer, Marcel Lajos [1902–81]: Hungarian Bauhaus-trained architect who also came to head its furniture department and designed stylish pieces such as the Wassily leather and tubular steel chair, and a soon-to-be standard 1928 cantilevered chair. His work has been influential to the present day thanks to its functional elegance and wide use of materials. The English Isokon Company made his 1935–7 bent plywood designs.
Brewster chair (1.05)
Bridal chest (1.16)
Brocade: multi-coloured silk fabric used for furnishings.
Broché work: a type of embroidery pattern, usually floral.
Broken triangular pediment (2.14)
Bubinga: West African hardwood similar to rosewood, mainly employed for veneer and inlay.
Bucranium: ancient Greek ox scull motif revived on neoclassical furniture from the late 18th century.
Buckle chair back (2.07), **Windsor chair** (1.14)
Buffet (1.31): table for serving meals, so called in the 16th century, usually multi-tiered. Replaced by sideboard but revived in Victorian Gothic period.
Buffet stool: late 16th/early 17th century joined stool.
Bühl: see Boulle.
Bulb turning (2.11)
Bulbous leg (2.10), **turning** (2.11)
Bullion fringe: heavy twisted cord hanging at the foot of a furnishing.
Bun foot (2.09), **turning** (2.11)
Bureau (1.23, 1.24): confusing and widely applied term. In France denoted all forms of writing furniture. In Britain specifically applied to slope-topped desks (45-degree angle when closed) with small drawers and cubbyholes inside and long drawers below. Sometimes a bookcase was added to the superstructure. The earliest surviving examples of this characteristic desk form date from the 1690s. In America such a desk was called a secretaire and bureau meant a chest of drawers, especially in the bedroom.
Bureau bedstead (1.01), **bookcase** (1.18), **Mazarin** (1.24), **plat** (1.24, 1.31), **table** (1.23)
Burl/Burr wood: tree trunk or root protrusion valued for its decorative grain when cut through for veneering. Walnut, yew, elm, maple and ash trees are particularly rich in burls.

Breuer: laminated plywood chaise longue c1930

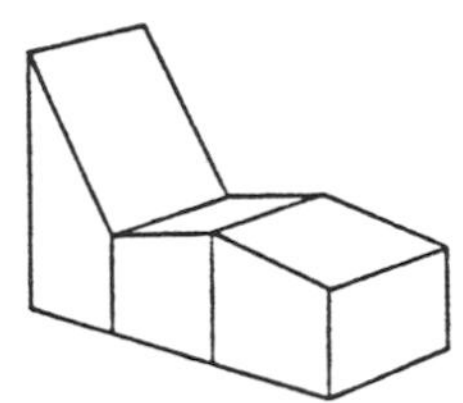
Burton: chaise longue

Byzantine: ivory cathedra throne of Bishop Maximianus of Ravenna c550

Burton, Scott [1939–89]: American designer and sculptor who began with bronze historical replicas before developing 1970s 'vernacular' chair sculptures. He designed striking 1980s permanent outdoor seating in stone for public buildings at Boston, New York and Liverpool.
Butler's table/tray (1.31)
Butt hinge (2.12), **joint** (2.15, 2.16)
Butterfly hinge (2.12), joint (2.16), **spline joint** (2.16), **table** (1.32)
Butternut: American white walnut hardwood that darkens with age. Due to scarcity, seldom a furniture wood since about the 1850s.
Byzantine chair (1.05), **furniture**: East Roman Empire furniture style based on Constantinople from the 5th to 15th centuries. Inherited and elaborated Early Christian and Hellenistic forms blending them with Persian, Islamic and even Chinese influences. Featured elaborate turnings; metal X-frame chairs; foot stools; lecterns; round or semi-circular dining tables; canopy beds; open and closed cupboards; separate bookcases in the late period; and elaborately decorated chests.
Cabinet (1.18), **on-chest** (1.19), **on-stand** (1.19): furniture with shelves and/or drawers for storage.
Cabinetmaker: a skilled furniture maker, especially with veneering.
Cabinet stand (1.32)
Cabochon (3.06): French Rococo-originated raised oval or spherical motif resembling a gemstone.
Cabriole chair (1.06), **leg** (2.10), **sofa** (1.25)
Camel back chair (2.07), **sofa** (1.25)
Campaign field bed (1.01), **escutcheon** (2.13): collapsible, portable furniture primarily for military use in the field or aboard ship. Surviving modern examples begin in the late 18th century.
Camp bed (1.01)
Canapé sofa (1.25)
Candelabrum (1.38): multi-branched candlestick or chandelier.
Candlebox (1.40): hanging wooden box for storing candles.
Candleslide (2.04)
Candlestand (1.29): small, usually tripod or four-legged, stand first made in the late 17th century. Also called *torchère*.
Candlestick (1.38): socket candle holder in wide use since the 16th century, usually made of metal.
Cane (2.07): chair seat and back material (rattan palms) copied from Indian furniture imported to the West by Portugal and first used in England under Charles II. Whole cane furniture was popular in later 17th century Anglo-Dutch homes and again from the early 19th century.
Canephorus: sculpted, usually female figure with a basket on the head, used in Louis XVI furniture for gilt-bronze mounts.
Canopy (2.01): a covering suspended over a bed or throne, see Tester.
Cant (canted) (3.05): furniture feet, legs, or angled corners sloping outwards, also a projecting form of chamfer or bevel.
Canteen: portable box for carrying cutlery and condiments.
Canterbury table (1.32)
Cantileveral chair (1.06)
Capital (2.14)
Capping: square or turned ornament.
Captain's Windsor chair (1.14)
Caqueteuse/Caquetoire/Conversation armchair (1.06)
Carcass/Carcase (2.04): basic frame of a piece of furniture.
Card cut: Chinese-style latticework ornament, practised by Chippendale.
Card table (1.32), **hinge** (2.12), **strap hinge** (2.12)
Carlton house table (1.32)
Carolean: King Charles II's reign (1660-85), another term for Restoration or late Jacobean work.
Cartonnier/Serre-papier: filing cabinet in French. From the 18th century a two-drawered or pigeonholed piece, either standing alone or on a *bureau plat.* Some even had a clock added.
Cartouche (3.06): tablet or scroll-like decorative motif derived from Roman designs and which first reappeared on 15th century Renaissance furniture. Frequently seen in the middle of a cabinet pediment, often inscribed
Carver chair (1.06)
Caryatid: sculpted female figure support, notably in Renaissance or neoclassical furniture.
Case: any box-like furniture.
Casket: small box for valuables.
Cassapanca sofa (1.25)

Cassone (1.16)
Cast-iron furniture: principally for garden, outdoor and public use. First generally made in Britain from the 1840s, Europe and America following suit.
Castellated: moulding pattern imitating battlements.
Caster/Castor: small pivoted roller wheels for furniture, invented in the 16th century.
Castle, Wendell [b1932]: American leader of the 1970s handicraft furniture revival with sculpted pieces of laminated wood.

Castle: laminated wood seating

Cavetto moulding (3.03), **pediment** (2.14)
Cedar: fragrant pale-brown softwood family particularly used for storing clothing. Lebanon cedar came to Britain in Charles II's reign.
Cellaret/Cellarette (1.16): deep drawer or cabinet on legs (both having a lockable lid) for storing and keeping bottles of wine or spirits cool, see Wine-cooler. Often metal-lined to take ice. In its separate form used pre-1700 to the late 19th century.
Centre drawer guide: wooden rail under a drawer's middle to help it slide.
Certosina work: bone, ivory, metal and mother-of-pearl inlay on dark wood in North Italian and Hispano-Moresque styles from the 14th to 18th centuries.
Ceylon satinwood: Sri Lankan hardwood, yellow to golden in colour. Used in Western furniture since c1800 and today's main commercial satinwood.
Chain (3.02): a form of motif.
Chairs (1.05-1.15): a raised single seat.
Chair backs (2.07-2.08): upright support for the sitter's back.
Chair back settee (1.26)
Chair table (1.06)
Chaise à la capucine (1.06), **à l'officier** (1.06), **courante** (1.06), **longue** (1.01), **meublante** (1.06)
Chamber/commode/Necessary chair (1.06)
Chamber horse (1.06)
Chamfer: corner edge at an oblique angle where two surfaces are cut away or planed.
Chandelier (1.38): multi-branched lamp or candle holder suspended from the ceiling. Wooden or iron ones used in Anglo-Saxon churches. Brass chandeliers joined by silver, glass (England from 1720s) and rock crystal designs during the 18th century.
Charles II/Restoration chair (1.06)
Chasing: engraving or embossing a metal surface with a rounded hammer or chisel.
Chatol desk/display cabinet (1.20)
Chauffeuse chair (1.06)
Cheesebox seat (2.03)
Chequer/Checker: chessboard pattern of decoration.
Cherrywood: prime furniture hardwood of attractive pale to red-brown colour that is strong and polishes easily.
Chest of drawers (1.16)
Chesterfield sofa (1.26)
Chestnut: pale, softish hardwood best used for inlay or veneering, most popular furniture application was early 18th century.
Chest-on-chest (1.16), **on-stand** (1.16)
Chests (1.16, 1.17): long rectangular storage furniture.
Cheval glass/Horse dressing glass (1.40): full length and tilting dressing mirror on trestles, often wheels. A 1790s neoclassical development that became the Napoleonic Psyche mirror. Made as late as 1910.
Cheval screen: two-legged fire screen and room dividers.
Chevron (3.01): a decorative motif.

Chinese Chippendale: china display case

Chiavari chair (1.07)
Chiffonier/Table en chiffonière cupboard (1.19)
Chiffonier/Chiffonière/Semanier chest (1.16)
Chimera (3.06): Greco-Roman mythical female and fire-breathing creature, popular adornment for Mannerist, 18th century and early 19th century furniture.
China cabinet (1.19), **table** (1.32)
Chinese back chair (1.07)
Chinese Chippendale (see style timechart): modern term for British 1750s and 1760s Rococo fashion in oriental ornament, as popularised by Thomas Chippendale, that featured pagodas and geometrical fretwork.
Chinoiserie: French word for European use of oriental motifs, particularly in the late 17th and throughout the 18th centuries.
Chintz: thin usually glazed calico cloth first imported from India in the mid 17th century. Used for drapes and seat covers.
Chip carving (3.06): simple geometrical work of the 13th to early 17th centuries. Chisel or gouge were the medieval tools used.

Chippendale: library breakfront bookcase 1762

Chippendale, Thomas [1718-79]: the household name of English furniture design who published *The Gentleman and Cabinet-maker's Director* (1754), the first exhaustive

Chippendale Gothic: chair pattern 1754

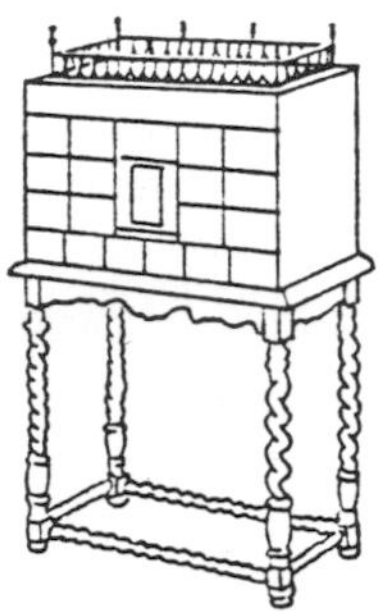
Churrigueresque: cabinet on stand late 17th century

Colombo: seating system 1968

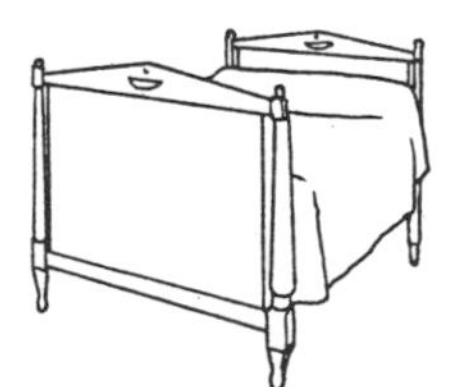
Consulate style: lit droit

catalogue (with 160 plates) devoted purely to furniture design. Chippendale's London business, carried on by his son Thomas [1749-1822], lasted over 70 years to produce Regency furniture. An organiser and master-designer, the elder Chippendale successfully adapted many styles beginning with French Rococo though specific Chippendale-manufactured furniture is both rare and hard to identify.
Chippendale Gothic (see style timechart): mid-18th century British Neo-Gothic furniture, using medieval architectural features.
Chromium plating: electrolysis process to coat another metal, giving a shiny finish and resistance to wear and tear. Especially used in modern tubular furniture.
Chuglam: Indian pale yellow hardwood with a decorative role, see Silver-grey wood.
Churrigueresque (see style timechart): lavishly exuberant Spanish Baroque style named after three prolific architect brothers. Its chairs were usually leather upholstered and the decoration's abundant inlaid features influenced Spanish Colonial patterns.
Cinquefoil: Gothic ornamental motif.
Clawfoot (2.09)
Cleat (2.04): a bracing strip of wood added to a flat surface to stop warping.
Clock bracket (2.05): a type of bracket.
Clothes press: early 18th century British shelved cupboard above a short chest of drawers.
Cloven foot (2.09)
Club sofa (1.26)
Cluster column leg (2.10)
Clustered columns: Gothic column with four or more jointly-sprung shafts.
Coaching writing desk (1.23)
Cockatrice (3.06): a decorative mythical serpent (basilisk).
Cock bead moulding (3.04)
Cock's head hinge (2.12)
Cocobolo: Bengali and Burmese dark wood of heavy and dense quality.
Coffee table (1.32)
Coffer: a transportable medieval chest, generally of leather-covered wood.
Coffre chest (1.16)
Coiffeuse chair (1.07), **table** (1.32)
Coin: English 18th century corner cupboard.
Coin cabinet (1.19)
Collar: a leg's horizontal moulding.
Collared toe: a wide-banded foot.
Colombo, Joe Cesare [1930-71]: highly original Italian 1960s designer famed for his multi-purpose Addition seating system and the first plastic chair to be made by one-process injection moulding.
Colonette: miniature ornamental column on furniture.
Column (2.14)
Columnar leg (2.10), **turning** (2.11)
Comb chair back (2.07), **Windsor chair** (1.14)
Commode (1.16), **clothes press** (1.16), **cressent** (1.17), **table** (1.17), **tombeau** (1.17): French for chest of drawers.
Companion chair (1.07)
Composite order: Roman combination of the Corinthian and Ionic orders of architecture.
Confessional armchair (1.07)
Confidante sofa (1.26)
Confortable armchair (1.07)
Congé: cavetto or ovolo moulding in furniture and architecture.
Connecticut chest (1.17)
Console: see Modillion:
Console bracket (2.05), **tables** (1.32)
Consulate style (see timechart): brief French transitional period named after Napoleon's term as First Consul. More formal and rectangular than the preceding Directoire pieces, introduced many of the military and Egyptian motifs that became common under the Empire. New forms were the *lit droit* and the *lit en bateau* (1.03).
Continuous arm Windsor chair (1.14)
Continuous coil spiral (3.01)
Conversation chair (1.06)
Coquillage: scallop-shell decorative motif.
Corbel (2.04): weight-bearing projecting bracket.
Corinthian order: third of the Greek architectural orders.
Corner basin stand (1.29), **block** (2.02), **cabinet** (1.19), **chair** (1.07), **cupboard** (1.19), **joints** (2.16)
Corner block (2.02): seating furniture triangular piece to join two sides and a leg below.
Corner furniture (1.07, 1.19, 1.29): piece to fit in a room corner.
Cornice (2.14)

Cornucopia: horn of plenty symbol used in many furniture styles since the Renaissance.
Coromandel lacquer: multi-coloured and carved Chinese lacquer and ebony folding screens exported from the late 17th century via India's east coast.
Coromandel wood: East Indies black-and-yellow striped ebony hardwood used for inlay or veneer, especially in 19th century Britain. Also called marblewood or calamanderwood.
Corona moulding (3.04)
Corridor stool/Window seat (1.26)
Cosy corner chair (1.26)
Cot bed (1.01)
Couch (1.02), **sofa** (1.26)
Couchette bed (1.02)
Cottage piano (1.39)
Countersunk and pellet surface (3.05)
Country Chippendale (see style timechart): late 18th century rural English and American simplified version of the main style using local woods rather than mahogany.

Country Chippendale: walnut serpentine front fall-front desk by J Shearer of Martinsburg, Virginia c1800

Court cupboard (1.19)
Cowhorn/Spur/Crescent/Crinotire (2.03)
Crapaud armchair (1.07)
Credenza cupboard (1.20)
Cressent, Charles [1685-1768]: leading French *Régence* and Louis XV cabinetmaker. Specialised in curved designs with gilt-bronze ormolu mounts. Devised the commode that bears his name (1.17) and concentrated on floral marquetry after c1750.
Cresset (1.38): pole-carried or wall socket-mounted open lamp with a spike mount for the candle inside the iron basket.
Crest rail chair back (2.07)
Crib bed (1.02)
Cricket stool (1.07), **table** (1.33)
Crochet surface decor (3.06)
Cross rail/Span/Slat rail: chair back's horizontal bar or rail below the crest rail.
C-scroll (3.06): a decorative motif.
Cromwellian chair (1.07)
Cross-lapped joint (2.15)
Cross rail (2.02), **stretcher** (2.02)
Crusie oil lamp (1.38)
Cucci, Domenico [1635-1704/5]: Italian Baroque furniture maker who lavishly furnished Louis XIV's palaces with extravagant pieces decorated by ebony, gilded and precious-stone studded pieces.

Cucci: cabinet for Louis XIV 1681-3

Cup, and cover turning (2.11)
Cupboards (1.18-1.22): case piece for storage.
Cupboard bed (1.02)
Cupid's bow: mid-18th century's chair back's top rail.
Cupped leg (2.10)
Curl veneer: wood veneer with feather cross grain.
Curule chair (1.07)
Cushion: variously-shaped stuffed bag of fabric for sitting or lying on.
Cushion capital: architectural feature of Romanesque furniture.
Cushion frieze: late 17th, early 18th century Anglo-American case furniture decoration consisting of a convex band of wood below the cornice.
Cusping: a pointed element with a Gothic arch, or in Gothic tracery.
Cut away escutcheon/backplate (2.13)
Cuvilliés, François the Elder [1695-1768]: Walloon-born Bavarian Rococo architect and designer who started as court dwarf to the Elector and went on to design Bavaria's finest Rococo palace interiors. The furniture was of a transformed bubbling Louis XV pattern which Cuvilliés detailed in engravings from 1738.
Cylinder: see Tambour.
Cylinder bureau (1.23)
Cyma curve device (3.06)
Cyma recta, reversa mouldings (3.03)
Dado joints (2.16)
Dagly, Gerhard [c1653-post 1714]: best known European white lacquermaker of his time. Used his Flemish home town Spa's black and gold colour scheme as well as brighter ones along with chinoiserie while working for the Elector of Brandenburg 1687-1713.
Dagobert chair (1.07)
Damascening: the art of inlaying iron (especially armour) with precious metals in arabesque. Strips were sold to cabinetmakers to decorate their pieces in late 16th century Milan whe ı Italian goldsmiths remastered this ancient oriental skill.
Damask: another craft originating from Damascus, a figured silk fabric, woven cotton or twilled linen with designs made vivid by reflected light. By c1250 well established in

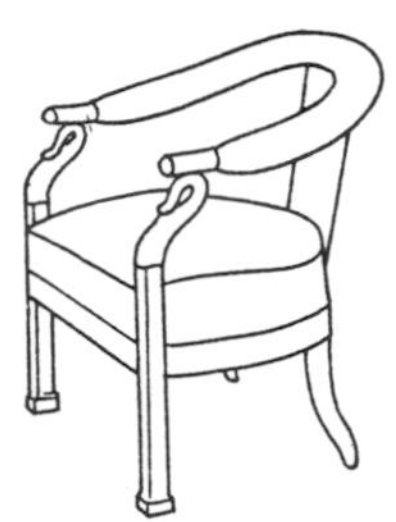
Danhauser: Vienna armchair 1820-30

Christendom as a furnishing product.
Danhauser, Josef [1780-1829]: leading Vienna workshop owner from 1804 who popularised the Biedermeier style. His company went on till 1838.
Danish Empire style (see timechart): early 19th century offshoot and prolongation of the French Empire style. Emphasised light marquetry and mahogany veneers with arched decoration. The Chatol cylinder-front desk (1.23) with display cupboards was the style's novel contribution.
Dante chair (1.13): see X-frame chair.
Davenport sofa (1.23)
Daybed (1.02, 1.27): platform for daylight resting.
Deal: English word for pine, especially the Scottish variety. Used since the 17th century as a carcase wood and as drawer linings.
Deception table (1.33)
Deck chair (1.07)
Demilune commode (1.17), **form** (3.05)
Demoiselle: woman's head-pedestalled French table for head dresses to stand on.
Denticulation: tooth-like classical ornaments used particularly on the cornices of 18th century case furniture cornices.
Dentil moulding (3.04), **pediment** (2.14)
Desk box (1.17), **chair** (1.07)
Desks (1.23-1.24): writing furniture.
Desornamentado style (see timechart): Spanish late-16th century reaction against excessive Renaissance decoration in architecture and furniture. The sparse furniture was allowed plain moulding, turned legs and panels. Lasted till the 19th century in Mexico and provincial Spain.
De Stijl (see style timechart): Dutch purist modernist movement that published a magazine of this title 1917-31. At least four members, especially Gerrit Rietveld (see entry), designed furniture on a rigorous application of an ideology based on the right angle and use of primary colours.

Desornamentado style: leather-backed chair of c1600

Deuddarn: Welsh court cupboard.
Deutscher Werkbund: German industrial design group of 1907-33 founded at Dresden. Its furniture practitioners included Van de Velde, Josef Hoffmann, Walter Gropius, Otto Wagner, Bruno Paul and Richard Riemerschmid. Immensely influential on the Modern Movement, and for the resolution of the conflicts between art and industry.
Deutscher Werkstatten: German reforming design movement stemming from an 1897 Munich workshop. The Dresden successor body, founded by a furniture maker, produced machine-made furniture in 1906.
Diamond point (3.06): a decorative motif, especially on both sides of the Channel in the early 17th century.
Diaper: ornamental chequered marquetry pattern of squares or diamonds continued from medieval furniture.
Dining chair (1.07), **table** (1.33)
Diphres and Diphros okladias stools (1.07)
Directoire (see style timechart): French Revolutionary furniture that reduced in scale and simplified the preceding Louis XVI style, especially in its late Etruscan phase. New daybed forms it introduced were the *Méridienne* (1.03) and the *Récamier* (1.28). The fasces and cap of liberty were important additions to the traditional classical ornaments.

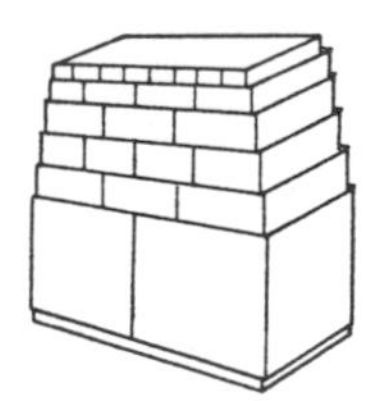
Deutscher Werkstatten: cabinet by Hoffmann

Director's chair (1.07)
Directory/American Regency (see style timechart): very early 19th century transitional phase between early US Federal and Empire style that drew on Sheraton's later ouput. Brought in paw feet, the Federal eagle, classical fluting and the Greek *klismos*.
Directory chair (1.08)
Dished corner (3.05): table corner hole for playing chips or money first seen on 18th century card tables.
Dishing (3.05): shallow depression in table surface as above, or in chair seats.
Distressed: an artificially or naturally aged piece of furniture.
Divan bed (1.02)
Dog rampant surface decor (3.06)
Dog's head couped (3.06)
Dog tooth motif (3.01)
Dolphins surface decor (3.06), **foot** (2.09)
Dome bed (1.02)
Domed pediments (2.14)
Doric order: the first order of Greek architecture.
Dorser/Dosser: pre-15th century fabric covering the back of seats or for a bed canopy.
Double cowhorn stretcher (2.03)
Double gate leg table support (2.06)
Double lyre stretcher (2.03)

Directoire: armchair

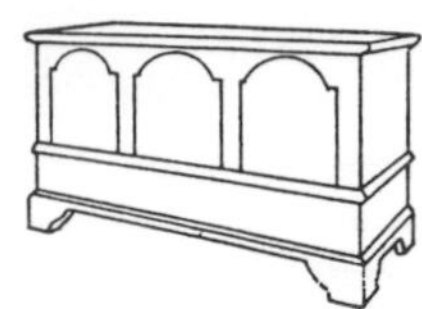
Dower furniture: Pennsylvanian German chest 1803

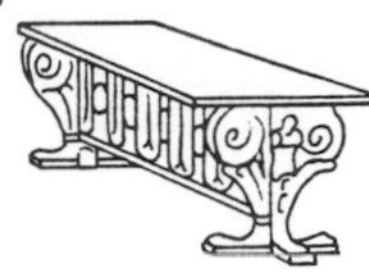
Du Cerceau: table with lion's paws c1550

Eames: swivel armchair 1956

Eastlake: Windsor chair 1872

Egyptian style: book cabinet

Empire: seat of Napoleon's throne, Fontainebleau c1805

Double arched and domed pediments (2.14)
Double cone motif (3.01)
Double twist turning (2.11)
Dovetail dado joints (2.16)
Dowel edge joint (2.16)
Dowel right angle joint (2.15)
Dower chest (1.17), **furniture**: domestic storage chests for a bride-to-be. Forms include Hadley chest (1.17), the *Cassone* (1.16) and German Pennsylvanian furniture.
Dragon surface decor (3.06)
Drake foot (2.09)
Drawer (2.05): sliding open-topped box in case furniture or below a table. Probably re-invented in 15th century Europe.
Drawer runner (2.05): Guidance rail for a drawer to run straight.
Drawing room chair (1.08)
Draw leaf (2.06): a form of table top, invented in the 16th century.
Draw slip (2.04): part of a cabinet or cupboard.
Dresser cupboard (1.20)
Dressing chest (1.17), **glass** (1.29), **mirror** (1.40), **stand** (1.29), **table/Poudreuse** (1.33)
Drinking table (1.33)
Drinks cabinet (1.20)
Drop front (Fall front/pull down front) (2.04): a form of table top.
Drop front desk (1.23)
Drop handle (2.13)
Drop leaf table (1.33, 2.06)
Dropped/scoop seat (2.03)
Drunkard's chair (1.08)
Du Cerceau, Jacques Androuet, the Elder [c1520-84]: French designer who published a pattern book (c1550) of Mannerist decoration and architectural furniture.
Duchesse brisée (1.26), **en bateau** (1.26)
Dumbwaiter/Lazy Susan (US) (1.29)
Dunand, Jean [1877-1942]: French Art Deco designer who founded a firm after 1918 to produce lacquered furniture, often decorated with precious metals or inlaid eggshell.
Dust board (2.05): panel between two drawers to exclude dust.
Dutch feet (2.09)
Eagle surface decor (3.06), **table** (1.33)
Eames, Charles [1907–78]: oustanding American modern designer renowned for his 1946 moulded plywood chair (1.08), a 1956 laminated rosewood and aluminium armchair, and modular storage units.
Ear: ornamental extension to a chair's crest rail, common in Chippendale and Windsor models.
Eastlake, Charles Locke [1836–1906]: British design writer whose *Hints on Household Taste* (1868) enjoyed enormous influence on both sides of the Atlantic.
Easy chair (1.08)
Ébéniste: French cabinetmaker of veneered case furniture. A guild job description abolished in 1791.
Ebonise: native hardwood stained to look like ebony, a technique used since c1800 as ebony became rarer and dearer, pearwood much used.
Ebony: deep black tropical hardwood used in antiquity by Egyptian and Mesopotamian makers. Use revived in 17th century Europe, but only a late 19th century American phenomenon. See Coromandel wood.
Edge joints (2.16)
Egg mouldings (3.01)
Églomisé: painting a glass door's reverse panel in blue, white and gold for decoration. This Roman glassware skill was revived by Louis XVI mirror/frame maker Jean-Baptiste Glomy.
Egyptian style/Egyptiennerie (see timechart): although interest in ancient Egypt was apparent by the 1760s, it was Napoleon's Egyptian Expedition (1798–9) which inspired Dominique-Vivant Denon's *Voyage in Lower and Upper Egypt* (1802), a richly engraved style book that shaped Empire and Regency furniture on both sides of the Atlantic. The Egyptian style was revived in the USA during the 1860s and 1870s.
Elbow chair (1.08)
Elephant trunk leg (2.10)
Elizabethan period (see timechart): see Tudor style.
Elm: light-brown hardwood used for furniture since Roman times. Notably the material for Georgian Windsor chairs and today's veneering.
Empire style (see timechart): virtually created by Napoleon's edict as First Consul (1801), it long outlasted Waterloo in Europe and America. Especially strong in furniture and furnishing, it emphasised martial glory, the letter N, Egyptiennerie, the swan (Josephine's

Etruscan furniture: bronze candelabrum

Etruscan taste: Adam piano wing for Catherine the Great of Russia before 1792

Fancy furniture: Fancy rocker by L Hitchcock, Conn c1830

Federal style: New York scrollback chair c1810-20

favourite), gilt bronze and mahogany. The *lit en bateau* (1.03), and the *lit droit* were widely used, while the full length Psyche mirror (Cheval glass) gained widespread currency in what was the golden age of the military tailor.
Encoignure (1.20): French corner cupboard, usually low.
Endive: modern word for 17th–18th century small Acanthus-leaf variant in decoration, much employed by Chippendale.
End joints (2.15)
End rail (2.01): part of a bed.
End scroll (3.02): a type of motif.
Enrichment: in furniture, specifically decorative inlaid or carved ornament.
Entablature (2.14): upper part of an architectural order.
Entasis (3.05): swelling at a column's middle to correct the optical illusion of it appearing hollow.
Ercolani, Lucien [b1888–19--]: Anglo-Italian maker and designer who founded Furniture Industries Ltd in the 1920s to produce Ercol traditional rustic pieces, in particular the Windsor chair.
Escabelle chair (1.08)
Escritoire desk (1.23)
Escutcheon: (a) a form of chair back taken from heraldic coat of arms (2.07). (b) decorative and protective surround or backplate to a keyhole or drawer handle (2.13).
Espagnolette (3.06): bronze female bust pillar support, common on Louis XIV, *Régence* and Louis XV pieces.
Etagère/what not stand (1.30)
Etruscan furniture (see style timechart): inventive pieces by this Greek-influenced Italian people included the woven basket chair; the unique *cista* round chest or casket; a solid tub-shaped armchair in bronze; bronze tripods and candelabra; and the placing of foot and head rests on the Greek *kline* (couch). See Roman furniture.
Etruscan taste: mistaken term for a Greco-Italian pottery painting style which inspired Neoclassical decoration introduced by Robert Adam in the 1760s. This terracotta, red, white and black colour scheme then features in Directoire furniture.
European redwood: North European softwood pine used for cheap furniture.
Extended/Extending table top (2.06): a table extendable by inserting an extra leaf or leaves.
Extension table (1.34)
Faldstool chair (1.08)
Fall front/Drop front/Pull down front desk (1.23): equipped with a hinged front for writing on when opened.
Fan (3.06, 3.07): chair back fan-shaped decoration used in 18th century work, upright or reversed.
Fan back Windsor chair (1.14)
Fancy furniture: US Federal period and after, light, ornamental furniture with plank, cane or rush seats. It was brightly painted or stencilled, Sheraton being the major design influence.
Farthingale chair (1.08)
Fasces: axe and rods carried by lictors before Roman Republican magistrates as the symbol of their authority. Common symbol on Louis XIV furniture and since.
Fascia moulding (3.03)
Faun: half man, half goat classical figure revived in Renaissance and Adam furniture.
Fauteuil chairs (1.08)
Favas: Louis XVI honeycomb decoration.
Federal style (see style timechart): American neoclassical style coinciding with the first generation of the new republic. Blended Anglo-French influences in mainly mahogany or fruitwood pieces. The American eagle was the outstanding decorative feature.
Feet (2.09): furniture supports.
Fernandino style (see style timechart): Spanish Napoleonic Empire-derived style named after King Ferdinand VII (1814–33). Its somewhat clumsy products boasted bronze mounts, giltwood appliqué and many classical symbols.
Ferrule: furniture leg's metal ring or cup, often fitted with a caster.
Festoon: a carved ornament of fruit and flowers as (a) a chair back (2.07) and (b) motif (3.02). Used in Renaissance furniture and since.
Fiddle back chair (2.07)
Field bed (1.02)
Fielded panel (3.05): panel made up of a number of small panels.
Filigree: delicate openwork gold or silver wire metal work in jewellery; any openwork decoration in furniture.
Fillet (3.03): a simple flat band that separates mouldings.
Finger end joint (2.15)
Finial (2.04): a vertical terminal ornament, often pommel or knob-shaped.

Finish: protective and decorative embellishment to the surface, eg paint, gilding, polishing (latter predominant by 16th century), lacquering and varnishing (both of 17th century origin).
Fir: coniferous tree wood used inside furniture due to its resinosity and softness.
Fire guard/screen: wire or metal mesh work (medieval cheval screen) to prevent fire sparks hitting those sitting by and to prevent children or pets falling in. Also an adjustable pole-mounted screen (17th century origin) with same function (1.38).
Firehouse Windsor chair (1.14)
Fishtail: top rail carving on a banister-backed chair.
Flambeau: flaming torch decoration.
Flat cornice pediment (2.14)
Flemish feet (2.09)
Flemish scroll (2.09), **leg** (2.10)
Fleur-de-lis: heraldic device and symbol of the Kings of France who had it applied to their furniture.
Fleuron: flower-shaped ornament.
Flower stand (1.29)
Flush bead moulding (3.04)
Fluted and square tapered leg (2.10), **torus moulding** (3.04)
Fluting (3.01): a form of motif common from the 16th century, especially in the last quarter of the 18th century. The opposite of reeding.
Fly rail (2.06)
Folding chair feet (1.02)
Fold over table top (2.06)
Foliated/Foliate leaf: foliage-like decoration.
Foliate and strapwork: see Laub und bandelwerk.
Fondeur-ciseleur: French metalworker and guild member (until the Revolution) who alone was allowed to cast and chase the metal mounts for furniture.
Foot: lowest part of a leg, often elaborately carved.
Footboard (2.01): part of a bed.
Footrail (2.02): part of a chair.
Foot stool (1.09)
Formica: trademark for a heat-resistant, easy-to-clean plastic laminate widely used on kitchen work surfaces. Normally about 1/16in thick and glued to plywood.
Four poster bed (1.02), **bedstead** (2.01)
Framing: skeleton of a piece of furniture.
François I style (see timechart): French Italianate style that made furniture more colourful and elaborately carved. It incorporated architectural elements, arabesque and Mannerist motifs. Walnut was the most common wood employed.

François I style: oak coffret c1530

French corner chair sofa (1.27)
French dovetail joint (2.16)
French polishing: heavily varnished multi-layered furniture process to provide a highly glossy finish. Technique originated in late 18th century France and is now often applied by machine.
Fret (3.01)/**Fretwork** (3.07)/**Fretting/Lattice work** : (a) forms of motif . (b) interlacing, geometrical straight line carved in metal or wood as low relief or perforated. Prominent in Rococo and Chippendale.
Fretted leg (2.16)
Frieze (2.14): the central area of an entablature, frequently used as an ornament on case furniture.
Frieze rail (2.06): part of a table and case furniture.
Fulcrum: Roman headboard on the reclining dining couch *(kline)*.
Fumed oak: oak yellow-tinted by ammonia fumes and especially favoured c1900–20.
Functionalism: modern doctrine of an object's use being the guiding design principle and the materials for it also being industrially produced, hence the creed of International Modern and Scandinavian furniture.
Gable: architectural three-cornered roof peak that appears on Romanesque and Gothic cupboards.
Gaboon: (a) poor mahogany from this region of West Africa. (b) the darkest ebony from the same area.
Gadrooning (3.01): see Nulling.

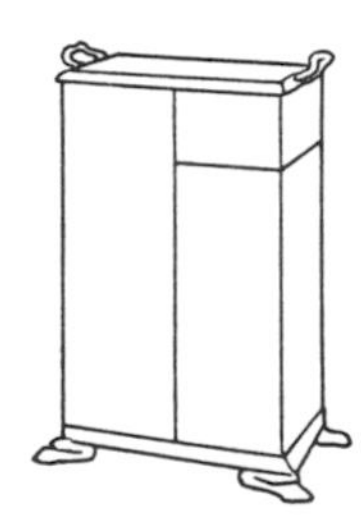
Gallé: marquetry umbrella stand c1900

Gallé, Emile [1846–1904]: French Art Nouveau glassmaker and founder of the School of Nancy, he also produced, with Louis Majorelle (1859–1926), a richly decorated furniture range after 1885 using many woods, natural ornamental themes and carved quotations.
Gallery (2.06): raised miniature fence-style border of metal or wood around a table top or that of case furniture in fretwork or balustrade form. The function is to stop small objects falling off.
Galloon: Anglicisation of French *gallon* (braid) meaning a upholstery or curtain trimming

in any of several textile forms.
Gaming table (1.34)
Garb (3.07): a type of surface decor depicting a corn stook.
Gate leg support (2.06)
Gentlemen's writing fire screen (1.38): small writing desk combining the function of a shield from fire while warming the toes. Thomas Shearer invented the type in Britain by 1788.

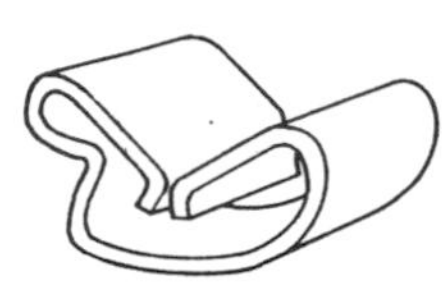
Gehry: cardboard chair

Georgian style (see timechart): term used in architecture to describe the range of late Renaissance English classical style, for furniture it encompasses at least nine styles. Its use reflects the fact that Britain's most famous designers (Chippendales, Adam brothers, Hepplewhite and Sheraton) flourished in the greater part of this regal era.
Gesso: a sizing and gypsum plaster that is applied thickly for carving, gilding and painting. Although of medieval origin, it was not much used in England until after 1700.
Gilding: decorating with gold dust or gold leaf which became popular for English furniture under Charles II (1660–85). Two methods: water gilding and oil gilding.
Gillow, Robert [1703–72]: founder (c1727) of a famous English makers that traded in Lancaster and London (Oxford St 1761–1906). Their records date back to 1731, most pieces being name-stamped after the 1760s. The company (Waring and Gillow) only closed in 1974 having employed Hepplewhite, as well as inventing the original billiard table (1760–70) and the telescopic dining table (c1800).
Giltwood: gilded wood.
Gimp/Guimpe/Gympe: upholstery trimming using narrow fabric, often to an openwork pattern.
Giraffe piano (1.39)
Girandole: a candelabrum; in England an ornamental Rococo single or multiple candle sconce (bracket) sometimes backed by a mirror.

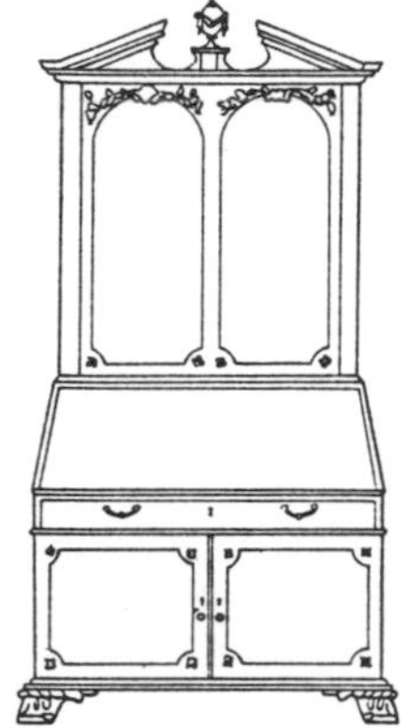
Georgian style: mahogany display cabinet and writing table c1760

Glasgow School (see style timechart): a group of designers centred around the Glasgow School of Art, and led by C R Mackintosh (see entry), his wife Margarat Macdonald, her sister Frances, and her husband Herbert MacNair. They were a major force in Art Nouveau handicrafts and architecture. The furniture was light, simple and open with Celtic motifs, being marketed in London from 1898.
Glastonbury chair (1.08)
Glazing bar (2.04): the metal or wooden members framing panes of glass in the windows of case furniture.
Glazing bead (2.04): metal or wood frame holding glass.
Globe stand (1.29)
Godwin, Edward William [1833–86]: British designer and architect who initially produced Neo-Jacobean furniture and c1861 switched to Japanese designs, creating a revolutionary Anglo-Japanese style (Oscar Wilde was a client) in the Art Furniture movement.
Gold leaf: a thin sheet of gold for gilding.

Gillow: slope top clerk's desk 1835

Gondola/Barrel/Tub chair (1.09)
Gothic back chair (1.09)
Gothic Revival (see style timechart): see Neo-Gothic.
Gothic scroll back chair (2.07)
Gothic style (see timechart): European furniture from the 12th to 16th centuries revived in the 19th century. Massive oak pieces centred on the chest, stonemasonry-style carving, arcading and vivid painting. Introduced the cupboard, wainscot chair, slab-ended stool/bench (15th century) and the linenfold motif.
Gothic Windsor chairs (1.14)
Gouge carving (3.07): simple medieval-style chisel pattern carving.
Gouty stool (1.09)
Gragg, Samuel [1772–1855]: an early American user of the bentwood technique who patented the 'Elastic' chair at Boston (1808–15).

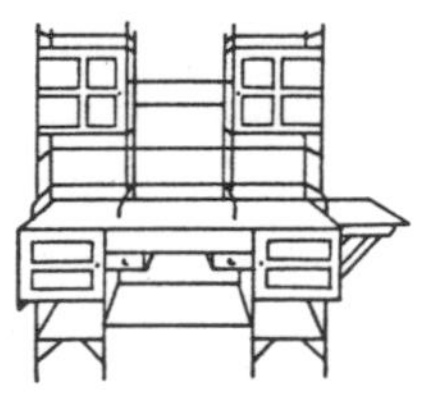
Godwin: ebonised Japanese-style cabinet 1877

Graining: painting that resembles wood.
Grand cottage piano (1.39)
Grape(3.01): an ornamental motif.
Grecian chair (1.09), **couch** (1.27)
Greek ancient furniture: almost none survives but artwork depictions do from the 9th century BC to the Roman end of the Hellenistic era. The couch (*kline*) was the outstanding item. Seating types included the *diphros* (1.08), *diphros okladias* (1.08), and the *klismos* (1.09), a Greek invention. Tables were small three or four-legged designs kept under the *kline*. The cupboard first appeared in Hellenistic times and the *kibotos* chest followed Egyptian precedent.
Griffin device (3.07)
Grille: ornament wooden or metal (brass or gilt) latticework protecting or replacing case furniture doors.
Grisaille: greyish-tinted painting to imitate carving, especially on neoclassical furniture (Adam and Sheraton designs in particular).

Gragg: bentwood chair 1808-15

Heal: bedroom cupboard and drawers

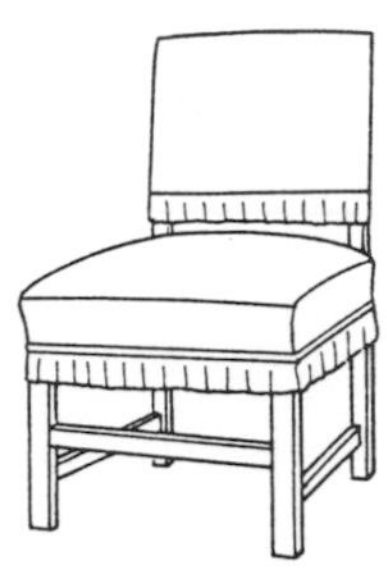
Henri II style: upholstered chair

Hepplewhite style: canopy bed c1789-94

High-tech/Industrial style: steel Accodata PC Mate stand with retractable keyboard shelf 1989

Gros point: wool on canvas cross-stitch embroidery in upholstery.
Grotesque sphinx device (3.07)
Guadamecil: tooled leather and sheepskin upholstery for Spanish Renaissance furniture, a Moorish craft in many colours named after Gadames in Libya.
Guard room table (1.34)
Guarea: mahogany-looking but stronger West African hardwood.
Guéridon stand (1.29)
Guilford chest (1.17)
Guilloche motifs (3.02)
Guttae motif (3.01)
Gumwood: furniture employs black gum, tupelo (see entry) and sweet varieties in cabinet work. They are strong, stainable but tend to warp unless heat-treated.
Gutta foot (2.09)
Hadley chest (USA) (1.17)
Half tester (2.01), **bed** (1.03)
Hall cupboard/Clothes press (1.20), **settee** (1.27)
Handkerchief table (1.34)
Handles (2.05, 2.13): furniture attachment.
Hanging cupboard (1.20)
Hanging shelves (1.40): wall shelving for books or china and particularly popular after c1750 when Chippendale Gothic and Chinese styles crossed the Atlantic.
Hangings: window, bed and portable wall textile drapery since the Middle Ages. Leather Spanish/Moorish hangings had their turn in the 16th and 17th centuries but the advent of wallpaper curtailed their use.
Hardware: any metal fittings on furniture.
Hardwood: wood from a broad-leaved tree, purely a botanical term.
Harewood/Greywood: dyed or stained sycamore or maple, an 18th century English inlay innovation.
Harlequin table (1.34)
Harvard chair (1.09)
Hasp hinge (2.12)
Hassock: a thick cushion or upholstered footstool, generally a church-kneeler.
Haster: an open-backed cupboard for warming plates. Gillow's records describe one in 1788.
Hat/hall stand (1.29)
Haupt, Georg [1741–84]: foremost Swedish 18th century cabinetmaker who trained and worked abroad before taking the Louis XVI style to Stockholm's royal court in 1769.
Hawk (3.07): a decorative device.
Hazel pine: British term for US red gum.
Head (2.04): part of a cabinet.
Headboard/Bedstock (2.01): part of a bed.
Headboard panel (2.01): part of a canopied bed.
Headrest: head support for a sleeper.
Heal, Sir Ambrose [1872–1959]: British maker and designer whose inherited London company was at the forefront of Arts and Crafts and Art Nouveau designs from 1893. Tubular steel was added to the range in the 1920s and Heal's son Christopher (b1911) became a leading International and Contemporary style designer from 1934.
Henri II style (see timechart): distinctly French 16th century Mannerist period that stresse bed carving, strapwork, arabesques, figurework and table pendant finials while lightening chairs and introducing the caquetoire armchair (1.06). See Sambin.
Hepplewhite style (see timechart): furniture produced to or similar to the designs of the London shop-owner George Hepplewhite (active c1760–86) whose posthumous *Cabinet-Maker and Upholster's Guide* (1788; revised editions 1789, 1794) contained almost 300 unsigned examples. Ten in a catalogue of the same year are his only signed work. Hepplewhite reinterpreted Adam's neoclassical style into a simpler, gentler-curved elegance. Serpentine and bow fronts, the shield-back chair (probably a Gillow's first), window seats, and Prince of Wales feathers are all characteristic.
Herculaneum chair (1.09)
Herringbone motif (3.02)
H-hinge (2.12), **stretcher** (2.03)
Hickory: US East Coast hardwood of light red colour, usually the material for Windsor chair back spindles and rails, as well as Adirondack furniture.
Highboy (US)/**tallboy chest** (1.17)
High chair (1.09)
High-tech/Industrial style (see timechart): international functional furniture design propagated in 1970s America that strives for novelty and ergonomic efficiency.
High Victorian style (see timechart): another term for Rococo Revival in Britain and America.

Hinges (2.12): furniture attachment.
Hip/Sitz bath (1.39): painted metal portable bath of early 19th century origin.
Hispano-Moresque style (see timechart): Mudéjar ('Moorish inspiration') geometrically-inlaid Spanish furniture of the late Gothic and Renaissance periods.
HL-hinge (2.12)
Hock leg ((2.10)
Hollow external joint (2.16), **moulding** (3.03)
Holly: speckle-grained, white hardwood used as a dyed substitute for ebony and for 18th century marquetry.
Honeysuckle ornament: see Anthemion.
Hood (2.04): desk part.
Hoof leg (2.09)
Hoop chair back (2.07)

Hope: circular table 1807

Hope, Thomas [1769–1831]: wealthy Scottish collector, designer and writer who pioneered Regency style and brought Egyptiennerie to Britain. Published the influential *Household Furniture and Interior Decoration* (1807).
Hoppenhaupt, Johann Michael [1709–55] and **Johann Christian** [1719–86]: German designer brothers who worked in Frederick the Great's palaces from 1740 and, with Johann August Nahl (1710–85), effectively brought Rococo furniture to Prussia. Johann Michael succeeded Nahl as the King's Director of Ornaments in 1746. The brothers favoured rich marquetry and plain veneer with chinoiserie. The elder Hoppenhaupt published his designs (1751–5).
Horn furniture: rural pieces made from animals' horns (1.09) since at least medieval times. Enjoyed a mid–19th century Anglo-German vogue, followed by a Wild West one in America.
Horse fire screen: see Cheval screen.
Horse rampant device (3.07)
Horseshoe-and-strap hinge (2.12)
Horseshoe dining table (1.34), **writing table** (1.34)
Hour glass seat (1.09)
Hunt board (1.34), **table** (1.34)
Hunt sideboard/Hunting board: higher, longer-legged and narrower than a sideboard, with drawers or cupboards; a case form special to horsemen of the American South either side of 1800 and usually made of walnut.
Hunzinger, George [1835–98]: American chairmaker and designer who founded his own New York firm in 1866 and patented over 20 designs. His chairs (1.09) were individualist creations in Revival styles with much turnery.
Husk: ornamental motif of small flowers in descending order, a popular classical device that came to England under Charles II.
Hutch cupboard (1.17)
Imbrication de (3.07)

Ince and Maythew: attributed semi-elliptical commode c1785

Ince and Mayhew [active 1759–1803]: successful London firm imitating and contemporary with Chippendale which published *The Universal System of Household Furniture* (1762) with 95 plates.
Indian laurel: dark hardwood with darker grain, mainly used for furniture in India although British 1930s veneering adopted it.
Indiscret sofa (1.27)
Inflatable furniture: air or water-inflated collapsible pieces popular since the 1960s, especially the water bed.
Initials (3.07): owner's or maker's names carved or inserted onto furniture.
Inlay: embedded design of different material in the primary wood, a craft since ancient Egypt.
Intaglio: opposite of relief carving, the design is cut below the surround.
Intarsia/Intarsio (Italian): wood or other inlay creating an architectural, abstract or landscape panel design; a luxury marquetry technique first practised in 13th century Siena and spread from Italy to South Germany and France after 1495.
Interlaced bow Windsor chair (1.14)

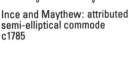

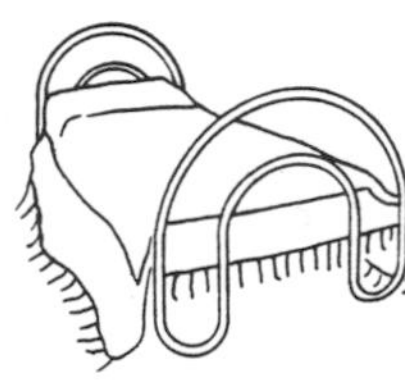
International style: English Practical Equipment Ltd bed 1932-6

International style (see timechart): European interwar style, so-called in 1932, that spread to America and the rest of the world. Its functional, often standardised furniture is made to this day.
Invalid/Bath chair (1.09)
Ionic order: second order of Greek architecture.
Iroko: African teak-like hardwood of yellow to brown hue, particularly in outdoor furniture.
Iron: used in furniture for ornamentation and reinforcement since Roman times, see Cast iron.
Iron wood: Brazilian hardwood of red-orange colour, a cousin of Brazilwood, that is best suited to veneering.

Jacobean style: court cupboard early 17th century

Jacob family: cradle of the King of Rome (Napoleon II) by F Jacob 1811

Jacobsen: Swan swivel chair 1958

Juhl: chair

Isabellino style (see timechart): Neo-Gothic/Rococo revival in mid–19th century Spain named after Queen Isabella (1833–68) that surpassed others in both colour and ornamentation (gilt and mother of pearl).
Isle of Man stretcher (2.03)
Ivory: elephant tusks (and those of other animals) carved as a furniture ornament since Old Kingdom Egypt. Especially a feature of Indo-Portuguese work and easily turned.
Jacobean style (see timechart): general term for 17th century English furniture at home and in America (see American Jacobean). Initially differed little from Tudor work until Continental-style arabesque carving, and Mannerist decorations grew in popularity. Upholstery and lightness became more general, as did the gate-leg table (1.34). The Commonwealth (1649–60) reduced decorating to a minimum, typified by the Cromwell chair (1.05), and is sometimes treated as a separate period. From 1660 (see Restoration style) England rejoined the European Baroque mainstream and began the Age of Walnut
Jacob family [active c1755–1847]: three-generation French furniture-making dynasty who span Louis XV to Gothic Revival styles. Georges (1739–1814), a *menuisier* from 1765, perfected the Louis XVI chair adding his personal marguerite symbol. He brought in English-style mahogany, the sabre leg, and the English lyre-back chair (1780s). Produced furniture for the Revolutionary government (1792). Father and sons (Georges 1768–1802 and François 1771–1841) combined to become the leading producers of Directoire, Consulate, and Empire furniture (Napoleon's palaces) even after the 1814–15 Restoration. Georges-Alphonse (1799–1870), son of François, continued the business until selling it in 1847 to Jeanselme whose own Second Empire-made name lasted until the 1930s.
Jacobsen, Arne [1902–71]: Danish designer (also an architect) best known for a 1952 stacking chair range (still made) and the sculptured plastic 'Swan' and 'Egg' chairs.
Japanese style (Japonism/Japonaiserie): late 19th century taste for Japanese art after trade resumed in 1853. Many major British designers, such as Godwin, adapted furniture to Japan's asymmetrical lightness and simplicity. Continental Art Nouveau makers took up the fashion in the 1890s and America was influenced from the late 1870s especially in bamboo work.
Japanning: lacquer-imitating Western varnish finish with gold painting against a black (or other coloured) background. The term arose because the best lacquer came from Japan but was rare and expensive (exported after 1650). A 1688 English treatise spread the skill so that New England too was well equipped to produce it by 1740. Japanning declined in the late 18th century, but revived in the mid–19th century. See Dagly, Lacquer and Vernis Martin.
Jardinière (1.29, 1.40) : large ornamented flower or plant stand (metal or wood) devised in 1760s France.
Jewelling: wood carving to resemble jewels.
Joiner: see Carpenter, Cabinetmaker.
Joinery (2.15–2.17): the technique of assembling wooden furniture.
Joint stool (1.09)
Juhl, Finn [b1912]: one of the first Danish Modern designers in the late 1940s.
Juvarra, Filippo [1678–1736]: Sicilian early Rococo architect and stage designer whose flamboyant furniture fills palaces he planned at Messina, Turin, Mafra (Portugal), and Madrid. He favoured exquisite scrollwork legs, figure supports and large pictorial inlays.
Kangaroo sofa (1.27)
Kast cupboard (1.20)
Katsura: Japanese hardwood employed as a plain veneer.
Keeftkast cupboard (1.20)
Keel moulding (3.04)
Kettle base front (3.05)
Key motif (3.01)
Kingwood/Violet wood: close-grained, dark purple veneering Brazil rosewood, especially in late 17th and 18th century work.
Kiri: silver-coloured Japanese softwood especially for constructing silk clothes chests.
Kline couch (1.03)
Klint, Kaare [1888–1954]: influential Danish Scandinavian Modern designer who headed the Copenhagen Royal Academy of Arts' new furniture department from 1924. He sought biotechnological 'tools for living' with plain woods, natural colours and without pretentious decoration.
Klismos chair (1.09)
Kneading/Bread trough (1.39): country piece of furniture for bread-making. French provincial examples are rich in decoration.
Knee: bulge of a cabriole leg.
Kneehole desk (1.23)
Knob (2.13): part of a door handle.
Knobbed butt (2.12)

Knoll Associates: plastic and foam Ottoman by Eero Saarinen 1948

Knoll Asssociates/International [active 1939–]: New York company who pioneered International Modern style designs by top names and marketed them internationally.
Knuckle: Terminating scroll on a Windsor chair arm rail.
Kunstschrank cupboard (1.20)
Kussenkast cupboard (1.21)
Kylix (3.07): a neoclassical surface decor motif depicting a Greek form of pottery drinking bowl. It appears notably on US Federal Hepplewhite chairs.
Laburnum: yellowish European hardwood employed for late 17th century and 18th century inlay and oystershell veneer.
Lac burgauté: applying mother-of-pearl fragments to lacquerwork, a Japanese skill (*Raden*) copied by 18th century Europe and also found in Art Deco pieces.
Lacca contrafatta: North Italian, especially Venetian, method of producing cheap imitations of lacquer by applying cutout prints to painted surface and then coating with clear varnish.
Lacquer & Japanning: Sino-Japanese tree sap, dissolved in alcohol, used to layer (or to make small items) metal or wood surfaces with up to 20 opaque coatings. Each is polished to produce a lustrous effect. Imported furniture led to Western imitations before 1614 (see Japanning) of this ancient oriental skill.
Ladder back chair (1.09), **chair back** (2.07)
Ladies' writing screen: a smaller version of the Gentlemen's writing screen (see writing).
Lambrequin (2.02): part of a chair imitating hanging drapery.
Lamp stand (1.29)
Landscape grain panel (3.05)

Lannuier: folding-top table

Lannuier, Charles-Honoré [1779–1819]: Parisian-trained American Empire style cabinetmaker, who emigrated to New York in 1803 and produced lighter Empire pieces with imported materials. He and Phyfe embody this American style.
Larch: light-red colour European softwood, an 18th century secondary wood.
Lath: backing strip to light furniture, eg Windsor and Deck chairs.
Lath and baluster, lath back Windsor chairs (1.14)
Lath chair back (2.07)
Lathe: machine for shaping turnery in use since the 9th century BC.
Lattice: open framework of wood or metal strips on case furniture or chair backs or pediments (2.14).
Laub- und-Bandelwerk: German for foliate and strapwork, a late Baroque arabesque decoration which flourished c1700–25.
Laurelling (3.07)
Leaf: additional section for extending a table top, either hung from hinges or slid below the main surface, or kept separately.
Leaf scroll foot (2.09)

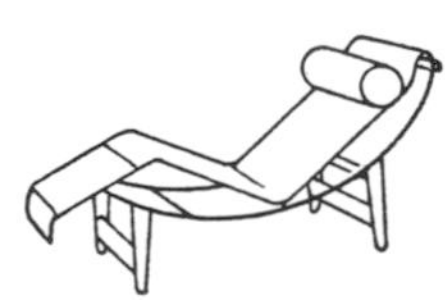
Le Corbusier: chaise longue 1927

Leather: used as furniture upholstery since the Egyptian Old Kingdom. Renaissance styles especially featured it with patterns of studded brass nailheads (English chair backs from c1645). Morocco goat leather was added to calf and oxhide in Louis XIV and Chippendale work. Treatments and decoration are multifarious.
Leatherette: a modern artificial leather made of cellulose-coated cloth.
Le Corbusier (Charles Edouard Jeanneret) [1887–1965]: pivotal modern architect who also designed furniture with his brother Pierre Jeanneret and Charlotte Perriand (1926–9) using leather and tubular steel to produce such classics as the adjustable Cowboy chair (a chaise longue) and the Grand Confort easy seat.
Lectern (1.30)
Leg and stretcher (2.06): furniture supports.
Legrain, Pierre [1889–1929]: the most avant-garde French Art Deco designer, primarily a bookbinder, whose 1920s furniture included African-derived stools, a glass grand piano and use of chromium, vellum and velvet.
Leg rest (1.40): furniture accessory since the early 19th century.
Legs (2.01, 2.02, 2.05, 2.06, 2.10): furniture support.
Leopard's face device (3.07)
L-hinge (2.12)
Liberty style: see Art Nouveau.
Library furniture (1.10, 1.18, 1.35, 1.40): pieces to aid study.
Lignum vitae: Central American and West Indian greenish-brown hardwood, the most durable known. Especially used in English late Stuart cabinet veneering.
Limed oak: oak treated with lime left in the grain.
Limewood/White or bass wood (USA): cream-coloured softwood ideal for carving as in Tudor and Grinling Gibbons' (active c1663–1721) work.
Liming: bleaching furniture with lime to lighten the wood colour before painting, a technique since the 16th century.
Linen/Card press (1.40): board joined by large screws for pressing sheets and table linen. Used in 16th century Italy, English Charles I examples survive and 18th century makers

Louis XIII style: cabinet

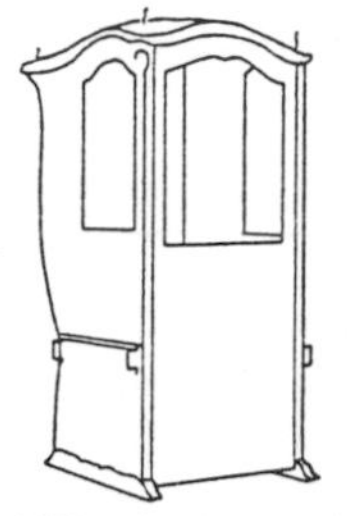
Louis XIV style: Sedan chair

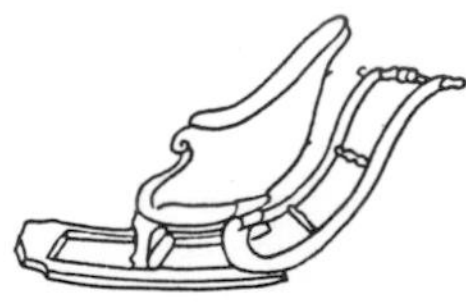
Louis XV style: sleigh in wood gilt

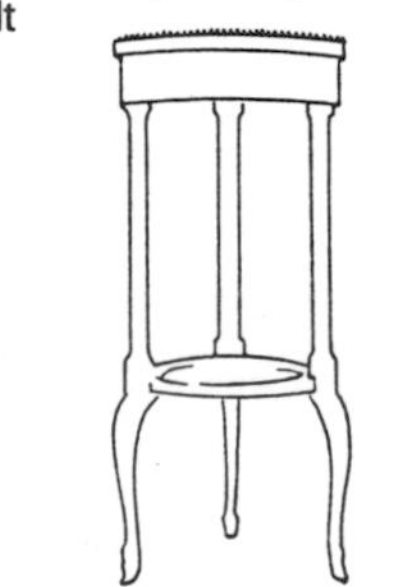
Louis XVI style: small tripod table

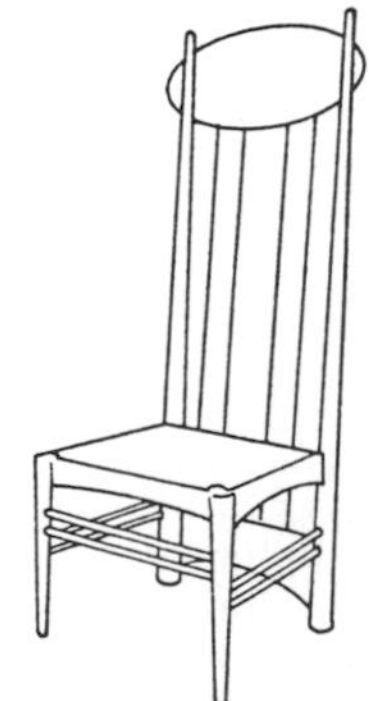
Mackintosh: high-backed side chair for Vienna Sezession Exhibition 1900

sometimes added them to chest of drawers.
Linenfold motif (3.01), **panelling** (3.05): also known as parchment
Lion devices (3.07), **escutcheon** (2.13)
Lits (French) **beds** (1.03)
Lobing: see Gadrooning.
Locker: originally a lock-secured chest or box. Now a smallish lockable unit in a set of changing-room lockers.
Lolling back chair (1.09)
Loop handle (2.13), **hinge** (2.12)
Loose slip seat (2.03)
Loo table (1.35) : originally used for the game lanterloo.
Loper (2.04): sliding supports for a drop front desk's writing surface (or for an extending table). They are extended manually or sometimes automatically by springs when the desk is opened.
Lotus motifs (3.02), **device** (3.07)
Louis XIII style (see timechart): early 17th century French furniture in showy Mannerist fashion and made of ebony or walnut wood, decorated with lavish semi-precious stones and veneering. Flemish-imported geometric panels are its most distinctive feature. The cabinet, the most important piece, sometimes had a fall front added thus becoming the *secretaire à abattant* desk (1.24). Mainly oblong-shaped tables abounded and dining tables first had extensions. Upholstery included leather and became fixed for the first time.
Louis XIV style (see timechart): France's Baroque period centred round the glorious reign of the Sun King in which the vast new Palace of Versailles (1668 on) was the apotheosis. Furniture formed part of an integrated royal programme of decoration in which magnificent but disciplined design enveloped the 20,000-member hierarchical court where even the size of foot stools was graduated. New and enduring furniture forms were the *canapé* sofa (1.25); the Confessional armchair (1.07); the *fauteuil* armchair (1.08); the console table (1.32); often marble topped; and the commode (1.16) which ousted the traditional chest. Chinoiserie joined the decorative repertoire from the 1670s, see Boulle.
Louis XV style (see timechart): the true Louis XV Rococo style occupies the middle years of that king's reign and is arguably furniture's richest period. The finest aristocratic homes had winter and summer sets of curving furniture, elegantly made from up to 50 types of wood that were carved and ornamented to the highest standards with metalwork, chinoiserie, gilt, mirrors, porcelain plaques and bright colours. The *bergère* easy chair (1.05), first made c1725, proliferated as did the cabriole chair (1.06) and the *duchesse*-type chaise longues (1.27). Desk choice widened with the cartonnier accessory, the first ever roll top model (1760–9) made for the King himself, and the mechanically ingenious dual-purpose *secretaire à Capucin* or *à la Bourgogne* (1750s).
Louis XVI style (see timechart): this reaction to Rococo flippancy predated and outlasted the King whose name describes it. Sparing neoclassical themes and straight lines returned. The cabriole leg was ousted by square or round-turned feet and then the sabre leg. Breakfront case shapes replaced the flamboyant bombé. Plain or pale colours supplanted brighter ones. More numerous skilled cabinetmakers obtained wider patronage. Three specialised types of commode appeared in the 1770s followed c1775 by the *bonheur du jour* (1.23), a popular cabinet-surmounted small writing desk.
Louis XVI Revival (see timechart): mid–19th century style that crossed the Atlantic from the court of Napoleon III and Empress Eugenie's Second Empire to Civil War-era America. More ostentatious than the original, especially in deep-button, coil-sprung upholstery. Widespread and prolonged use in burgeoning grand hotels across the world led to its description as 'Louis the Hotel' style.
Loveseat sofa/Courting chair (1.27)
Lowboy chest (1.17)
Low post bed (1.03)
Lozenge motif (3.02): diamond-shaped device (from heraldry) often featured in diaper work (see entry).
Lug support (2.04): part of cabinet construction.
Lunette motif (3.02)
Luther chair (1.13): see X-frame chair.
Lyre back chair (1.10)
Lyre device (3.07)
Mackintosh, Charles Rennie [1868–1928]: Scottish Art Nouveau designer who made furniture for his buildings in partnership with his wife Margaret Macdonald, notably for the Glasgow School of Art and for several Glasgow tea-rooms (c1897–1912). At 1890s Paris and Munich exhibitions he strongly influenced European design trends.
Magazine rack stand (1.29)
Magnolia: American tulip tree pale hardwood chiefly used for frames and linings.
Mahogany: key English furniture material since the 1720s when walnut became scarce.

This richly red (when polished) beautiful and strong hardwood was first imported from Cuba and Honduras (Spanish Renaissance examples). It became synonymous with dining table in the Age of Mahogany. South American species appeared on the market in the early 19th century (see African mahogany).

Mannerist style (see timechart): European fashion of Italian origin in the late 16th and early 17th centuries. Emphasised arabesque and grotesque ornament. Special furniture forms were the French *table à l'Italienne* (1.36) and the German *Kunstschrank* (1.21). The even more serpentine Auricular phase (see entry) prevailed until the coming of Baroque. See Du Cerceau and Vredeman de Vries.

Mantel: lodge or shelf above a fireplace and also its surround named after the horizontal timber across the chimney breastwork. The term can be traced back to 1624. During the 18th century it became an elaborate wooden decorative furnishing to a room.

Maple: North American hardwood of light yellowish colour with a smooth and varied texture. Rapidly used for furniture by the early colonists.

Marble: furniture material since ancient Egypt and revived in the Renaissance. The Louis XIV and XV styles used it for surfaces. England joined the fashion after 1720 including coloured marbles (c1738) and semi-precious varieties (1750s). Neoclassical imitation marbles caused its use to diminish, but the Empire style ensured its popularity for the rest of the 19th century in Europe and America, notably the grey and white pattern.

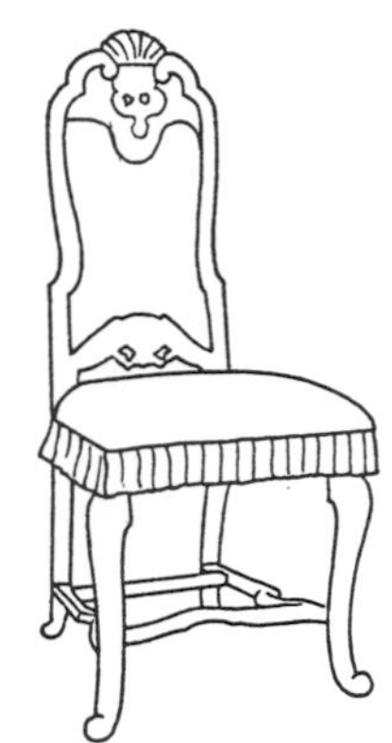

Marot: Dutch Marot-style chair after 1685

Marbling/ Marbleizing: simulating marble on wood or paper. The latter, a Persian skill, came to 16th century Europe via the Ottoman Empire.

Marchand-mercier: an 18th or 19th century French furniture dealer who often had an international clientele, employed cabinetmakers, and furnished palaces.

Marguerite: decorative motif of a daisy or similar petalled flower, the craft mark of Georges Jacob on Louis XVI chairs.

Marlborough leg (2.10)

Marot, Daniel [1663–1752]: Dutch Baroque architect and designer, of French Huguenot family, who translated Louis XIV Baroque to William and Mary whose court architect he became. Visited England (Hampton Court Palace) 1694–8. May have originated the design of the standard William and Mary chair and his engraved designs (1702) influenced elaborate beds, tables and guéridons.

Marquetry: contrasting wood(s), or other materials, inlaid into veneered wood, especially on case furniture. A technique of antiquity revived in Renaissance Italy (see Intarsia).

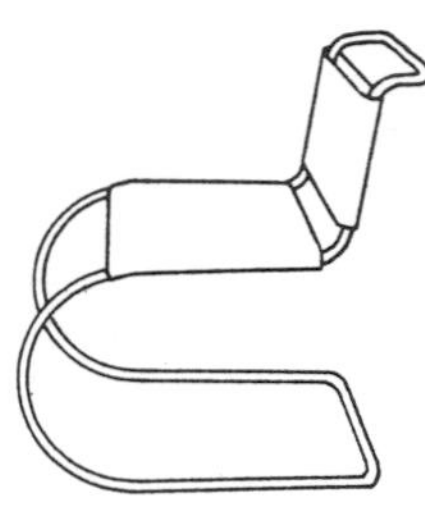

Mies van der Rohe: tubular steel chair 1927

Marquis chair (1.10)

Martha Washington chair (1.10)

Martlet device (3.07)

Mask: surface décor device of a grotesque human or animal face.

Matt gilding: 18th century dull finish to bronze fittiings.

Matting: surface décor device of a pattern of circles or dots used as background.

Mattress: a bed furnishing of variously stuffed cloth.

Medallion: variously shaped plaque with carved or painted decoration.

Mission furniture: oak sofa

Melon bulb leg (2.10), **foot** (2.09), **turning** (2.10)

Member: a single structural part.

Mendlesham Windsor chair (1.15)

Menuisier : French joiner who made tables, chairs and other solid items without veneering, the latter craft being the preserve of the *ébéniste* until 1791.

Mercury gilding: dangerous toxic process of covering bronze ormulu work with gold, outlawed by the French Revolution.

Méridienne bed (1.03), **sofa** (1.27)

Mermaid device (3.08)

Middle lap joint (2.15)

Mies van der Rohe, Ludwig [1886–1969]: German-American International Modern architect and designer who designed cantilevered tubular-steel furniture from 1926 culminating in the revolutionary 1929 Barcelona chair. Knoll International reissued his elegant work in the 1950s.

Milking stool (1.12)

Millwork joint (2.16)

Mirror (1.40): a looking glass. Metal types were only gradually superseded by larger glass ones from 1564 (Venetian mirrormakers' corporation) until they became major factors in interior design.

Misericord seat (1.10)

Mission furniture (1.10): American style arising from the British Arts and Crafts Movement (see entry) which inspired Gustav Stickley (1854–1942) to found his own New York firm (1898–1915). It made simple, massive oak pieces with cloth, canvas or leather upholstery as did the Royston Community (1895–1938). Stickley's magazine *The Craftsmen* (1901–15) spread the gospel of utility of design to the West Coast.

Mitred joints (2.15)

Mixing table (1.35)

Morris and Company: oak cabinet c1865

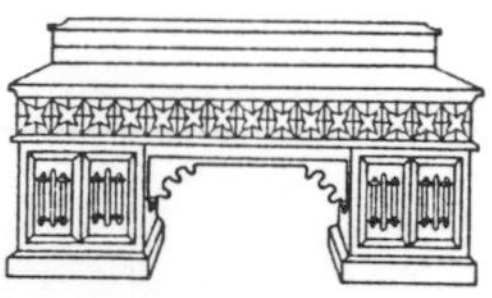
Neo-Gothic style: sideboard design by Loudon 1833

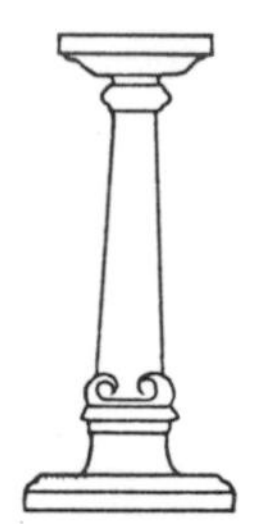
Neoclassical style: stand by J F Neufforge 1765-8

Newport Chippendale: blockfront kneehole desk attributed to John Townsend 1770

New York Chippendale: mahogany side chair 1760-80

Modillion: architectural cornice support transferred to neoclassical case furniture.
Monopod: Roman-inspired neoclassical table or chair with single support in animal form, prominent among French Empire and British Regency work.
Moon (1.38): spherical lantern holder on a pole, of 16th century origin.
Moore, James [c1670–1726]: English Baroque cabinetmaker in royal service from c1708 who specialised in gilt gesso and carved work. Made furniture at Kensington and Blenheim Palaces to the architect William Kent's designs. A silver table, sconces and mirrors of his survive at Erthig, North Wales.
Moorish style (see timechart): long-lasting Islamic Iberian style created by the ruling Moors who invaded from North Africa and were brilliant woodcarvers and leatherworkers. Little furniture was used or survives from this era in which richly-covered cushions were more important, but it was part of the Muslim world inspiration for a 1856–1907 revival. See Mudéjar.
Moresque: see Arabesque.
Morris and Company [1861–1940]: craft co-operative founded by the writer and designer William Morris as the centre of his Arts and Crafts movement. It produced simple streamlined furniture which was painted with medieval scenes by Pre-Raphaelite artists. See Webb.
Morris chair (1.10)
Mortise: wood cavity to receive projection of the same shape, a fundamental part of joinery.
Mortise and tenon joints (2.17)
Mother-of-pearl: oriental use of a polished inner shell layer copied in European furniture inlay since the 17th century.
Motifs (3.01, 3.02): standard running ornamentation.
Mottled: blotches or spots on veneering.
Mouldings (3.03, 3.04): a type of decoration and finish mainly derived from architecture.
Mudéjar style (see timechart): Spanish-Moorish synthesis that features complex geometric work by those Muslims 'permitted to remain' after the Christian reconquest.
Mule chest (1.17)
Mullion/Muntin: vertical border to a panel of glass, see also Glazing bar.
Muninga: variously coloured East African padauk hardwood used for construction and veneering.
Music furniture (1.21, 1.29, 1.30): aids to playing music.
Myrtle: Pacific coast yellowish wood ideal for veneer and inlay work.
Nailhead motif (3.01), **moulding** (3.04)
Nails: used to secure and decorate upholstery, especially in Iberian and Henri III styles.
Necking: any moulding or bead on a vertical support in furniture.
Needlepoint: embroidered canvas upholstery.
Needlework: hand embroidery of all types.
Nelson/Trafalgar Windsor chair (1.15)
Neo-Gothic style/Gothic Revival (see timechart): historicist, romantic and catholic attempt to revive Gothic medieval art from the late 18th to the end of the 19th centuries. The first furniture designs were published in 1742, influenced Chippendale, and produced the Gothic Windsor chair (1.14), popular for two decades. Regency Gothic (see entry) preceded the stronger 19th century revival which swept the Continent during the 1830s and dominated American work 1830–80 ending with the Eastlake phase.
Neoclassical style (see timechart): furniture of Greco-Roman inspiration (archaeological discoveries from the 1740s) from the 1760s to the 1830s embracing many different national styles.
Nest of drawers: late 17th and 18th century description for a tiny chest of drawers.
Nest of tables (1.35): a set of three or four tables of graduated size so that they can be stored under each other.
Newport Chippendale (USA): Rhode Island work of c1755–90 mainly by the Townsend-Goddard dynasty, simpler and less ornamented than the contemporary Philadelphia output.
New York Chippendale (USA): New York City work of c1755–90 distinguished by square ball and claw feet, nulling and the absence of case furniture.
Niche: a shallow, ornamental recess.
Nonsuch chest (1.17)
Notching: primitive woodwork decoration.
Nulling/Gadrooning (3.08): a type of surface décor with alternating fluting, especially on 17th and 18th century table and cabinet edges.
Nursery chair (1.10)
Oak: pale yellow European and American hardwood of which most furniture was made before the mid–17th century.
Occasional tables (1.35)
Octagonal escutcheon (2.13)

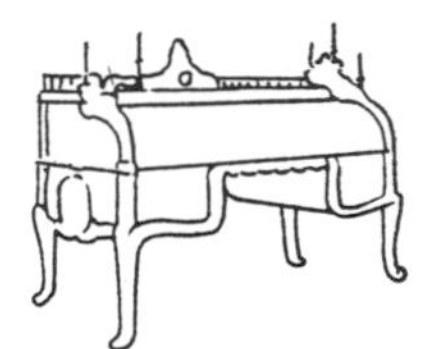

Oeben: roll top desk for Louis XV 1760-9

Palladian style: carved and gilt armchair by Kent c1731

Oeben, Jean-François [1721–63]: French Louis XV and Transitional style maker trained by Charles Boulle and patronised by Madame de Pompadour from c1745. He succeeded Boulle as royal cabinetmaker in 1753 and specialised in mechanically-fitted pieces, culminating in his novel roll top desk for the King (1760–9), see Riesener.
Ogee foot (2.09), **moulding** (3.04)
Olive wood: yellow to greenish-brown European Mediterranean hardwood, easy to polish and veneer.
Open padded chair back (2.08)
Open twist turning (2.11)
Openwork: pierced carving with complete openings.
Ormolu: gold-finished cast bronze ornament, literally 'ground gold', at its finest in French 18th century and Empire work.
Ornament: applied or carved decoration.
Ottoman sofa (1.27)
Oval back chair (1.10)
Oval handle (2.13), **escutcheons** (2.13)
Ovolo moulding (3.03)
Ovangkol: West African walnut-looking hardwood, a veneer and flooring material.
Oystering/Oystershell : a veneer taken from cuts of the grain in small trees to form patterns like oyster shells, a 17th century Dutch technique taken up by Restoration England for doors and drawer fronts. Burr walnut veneering replaced it in the 18th century.
Oxbow front: 18th century case furniture concave in the centre and convex to either side, the reverse of serpentine.
Padauk: wide range of red tropical hardwoods used since the 17th century in all parts of Western furniture (see Amboina wood).
Paldao: Philippines and New Guinea grey-brown coloured and dark-striped hardwood employed as veneer.
Palisander: Anglicisation of French for rosewood, particularly the dark-striped hardwood employed as a veneer.
Palladian style (see timechart): first distinctive British Georgian style designed by the architect William Kent. His furniture combined lavishly-sculpted Italian Baroque models with symmetrical ornament to match the interior designs. Kent's work was published in 1744.
Panel/Panelling (3.05): board inserted into a grooved frame either sunken below, flush with or raised above it. Became popular with 17th century Dutch furniture.
Panga panga: dark but streaked hard wood from East Africa used by Europeans for framing and veneering.
Papier-mâche seat (1.02)
Papyrus motif (3.02)
Parana pine: Brazil softwood of light colour and even texture employed for drawers and as a secondary wood.
Parcel gilt: part gilding on ornamental details.
Parlour chair (1.10)
Parquetry: wooden mosaic on furniture or floors in geometric patterns, at its finest in the Rococo.
Partner's desk (1.24)
Partridge wood: dark hardwood from Brazil with mottled streaks similar to the bird's. A particular feature of 17th and 18th century Anglo-French inlay details.
Pastiglia: gesso-like material for Italian Renaissance moulding on chests and boxes which was then gilded or painted.
Patent furniture: American furniture novelties, generally multi-purpose with moving parts, registered as new inventions, such as 1860s Platform rocker.
Patera device (3.08)
Patina: the sheen in furniture from polishing and age.
Pattern book: volumes of furniture designs, the first of which appeared anonymously in 1530; a highly influential and traditional method of spreading particular styles. Mass production and photography have now supplanted them.
Paw foot (2.09)
Peardrop motif (3.01)
Pear foot (2.09)
Pear shape drop handle (2.13)
Pearwood: a rare red-tinged North European and American hardwood, primarily for marquetry and inlay.
Pedestal (2.14), **cabinet**(1.21), **chair** (1.10), **desk** (1.24), **stand** (1.30), **support** (2.06), **table** (1.35)
Pediments (2.14): Renaissance furniture imitation of Greco-Roman architectural gable that appears unbroken c1675–1760 and in broken form c1715–1800.

Pennyslvania German: painted chair c1810

Philadelphia Chippendale: mahogany chest on chest (highboy) 1760–80

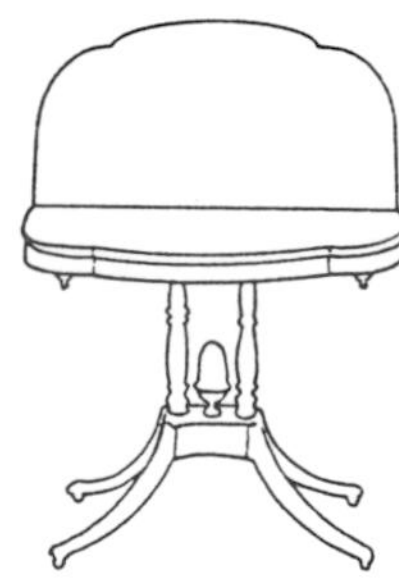
Phyfe: card table

Piffetti: cabinet/drawing table, Palazzo Reale, Turin c1732

Pelican device (3.08)
Pelmet (1.40): late 17th century development for framing a curtain rod with a fabric-covered board. Its border can be shaped and trimmed.
Pembroke table (1.35)
Pendant finial (2.04)
Pennysylvania German/'Dutch' (USA): 18th and 19th century softwood local style retaining European Baroque features, especially the Schrank wardrobe and the softwood chest with their folk decoration.
Pew (1.10)
Philadelphia Chippendale (USA): Pennsylvania's capital's style of c1755–90 rich in Rococo carving and fluted colonettes on cabinets.
Phyfe, Duncan [1768–1854]: foremost American Directory and Empire cabinetmaker at New York after c1792. He simplified Sheraton's designs in particular, preferring veneering to carving (except fluting and reeding) and delighting in paw feet. Modified the curule chair (1.07). Switched his 100-strong workshop to Pillar and Scroll rosewood work after c1830, retiring in 1847 with a $500,000 fortune.
Piano hinge (2.12), **stool** (1.10)
Pickled finish: whitish finish on stripped woodwork because some plaster filling and liming (see entry) remains.
Pierced bracket (2.05): a type of bracket.
Pierced carving: cut-through carved material.
Pierced cross stretcher (2.03), **escutcheon** (2.13)
Pierced splat chair back (2.08)
Pier table (1.35)
Pietre dure: Renaissance inlay form (from 16th century Italy) using marble and semi-precious stones.
Piffetti, Pietro [1700–77]: Italian Rococo maker who worked at Turin for the Piedmont royal court from 1731, producing luxuriously elaborate pieces with much ivory inlay and bronze mounting. The Quirinale Palace, Rome, also has his creations.
Pigeon hole (2.04): part of a desk.
Pilaster (2.06): a type of table support.
Pilgrim furniture: see American Jacobean furniture.
Pillar and scroll/American Restoration style (USA): brief imitation of France's post-Napoleonic fashion, emphasising pillar feet, scroll brackets and arms. Documented by John Hall's 1840 pattern book.
Pillow top chair back (2.08)
Pine: softwood traditionally used for everyday furniture and easy to carve, hence its use as carcasing for British 18th century walnut and mahogany pieces.
Pin hinge (2.12)
Piretti, Giancarlo [b1940]: Italian designer whose 1969 Plia folding chair of chrome and metal with plastic moulded seat has become an office furniture standard.
Pitch pine: strong American yellow softwood, widely supplied for 19th century school and ecclesiastical fittings.
Placet stool (1.10)
Plain curved and ring handles (2.13)
Plane wood: European pale-brown hardwood used for inlay and panels.
Plank seat (2.03)
Plant stand (1.30)
Plaque: metal or porcelain medallion set in neoclassical furniture.
Plastic furniture: versatile synthetic material used since 1945 especially for institutional furniture. Eames and Saarinen were the design pioneers.
Plate cupboard (1.21)
Plateresque style (see timechart): early 16th century Spanish Renaissance style derived from silversmith work decorating simple furniture shapes with geometric intricacy.
Platform bed (1.03), **rocker** (1.11)
Plinth: the projecting solid base of case furniture and also pillar base mouldings.
Plum: buff-coloured European hardwood used for medieval to 17th century everyday furniture plus marquetry in later periods.
Plywood: multi-layered compound of wood veneers, stronger and more flexible than any single wood variety. Limited 18th century use became popular with Belter's (and others) bentwood (US 1865 patent). Eames pioneered the post–1945 plywood moulding revolution.
Pole screen (1.38): see Fire guard.
Pop Art furniture: 1960s humorous reaction against the austere domination of Scandinavian Modern. Used vivid colours and consumer symbols.
Poplar: wide variety of Northern hemisphere white hardwoods, used for homemade work and 16th–17th century inlaying.
Poppyhead device (3.08)

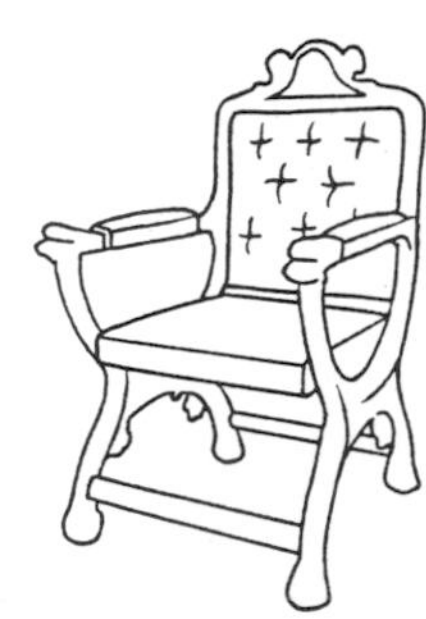
Pugin: armchair for Scarisbrick Hall, Lancs 1835

Pulpit: Romanesque, Bitonto Cathedral SE Italy c1200

Queen Anne style: walnut chest on stand soon after 1700

Porcelain: white ceramic ware first used as decorative plaques on French Rococo pieces from c1750, then appears through the neoclassical period and again in the Renaissance Revival.
Porter's chair (1.11)
Portfolio stand (1.30)
Post (2.05)
Pot board (2.04): part of a cabinet.
Pot table (1.30)
Pouch table (1.35)
Pouf stool (1.11)
Press cupboard (1.21)
Prie dieu (1.40), **chair** (1.11)
Prince of Wales feathers (3.08), **chair back** (2.08)
Print cabinet (1.21)
Pugin, Augustus Welby Northmore [1812–52]: seminal British designer who worked with his father on Regency Gothic furniture and published *Gothic furniture in the style of the 15th century* (1835). Produced 1200 pieces for the Houses of Parliament from 1840.
Pull down front/Drop front/Fall front: desk equipped with such a front for writing on.
Pulpit (1.30): internal or external elevated church platform for reading or speaking from. It is sometimes multi-storeyed and/or canopied. True pulpits started in Italy c1200.
Pulvinated frieze (2.14)
Purdonium/Purdonian (1.38): mid–19th century term for a coal scuttle with removable lining and rear socket for a small shovel.
Putto: decorative cupid motif employed since 15th century Italian Renaissance furniture.
Quadrant drawer (2.05), **hinge** (2.12)
Quadrant stay (2.04): curved metal support for a fall front desk front of Anglo-American neoclassical type.
Quaker chair (1.11)
Quatrefoil: Gothic furniture ornament, common in Revival work.
Queen Anne style (see timechart): distinct British national Baroque style of the 18th century's first quarter. Key elements included the cabriole leg (2.10); the drop handle (2.13); figured walnut veneering; fiddle back chair backs (2.07); and minimal carved decoration. Better joinery eliminated stretchers. New forms introduced were the china (display) cabinet (1.12), spoon back chair (1.14) for more comfort, the card table (1.32), the tea table (1.37), and the kneehole desk c1710 (1.23). See American Queen Anne style.
Queensland maple: tropical Australian rust-coloured hardwood, a mahogany look-alike used for construction there and as a polishable veneer elsewhere.
Queensland walnut: Australian hardwood of grey to brown appearance, a walnut look-alike used for flooring and case furniture there, also a popular British Empire 1930s wood.
Quirk: narrow groove in a moulding (3.04) or a mitred joint (2.15).
Rabbet/Rebate: woodwork-joining rectangular groove.
Race, Ernest [1913–63]: British Contemporary Style designer whose demountable 1945 BA chair was the first to use cast aluminium. His 1950 Antelope chair was similarly innovatory as his company, Race Furniture, remains.
Rack: frame or stand for many specialised roles, eg music (1.29), books, magazines, hats, letters or spoons.
Radiates: the rays of inlaid or carved fan or shell motifs.
Rails (2.01, 2.02, 2.04, 2,05, 2.06): parts in construction.
Rain mottle: a type of mahogany figuring.
Rake: an upright part's inclination from the vertical.
Ramin: white Indonesian hardwood, strong and light, a furniture material since c1950.
Ram's horn arm (2.02)
Rat tail hinge (2.12)
Rattan: South Asian climbing palm used for European cane furniture since the early 19th century.
Reading chair (1.11)
Reading seat sofa (1.27)
Rebate: see Rabbet.
Récamier daybed (1.03), **sofa** (1.28)
Recessed carving: 17th century English technique of emphasising the design by a textured, shallow receding background.
Recessed stretcher (2.03)
Réchampi: French decorative term describing painted or gilded work against another background colour.
Red gum/Satin walnut (UK)/**Hazel pine** (UK): smooth US hardwood much favoured for Hudson valley case furniture and much imported to Britain c1900–50.
Redwood: Californian softwood whose durability is exploited for outdoor furniture and

the burls of which provide table tops and veneering.
Reeded cup handle (2.13), **leg** (2.10), **torus moulding** (2.03)
Reeding (3.01): convex ridging decoration especially for neoclassical table and chair legs, the reverse of fluting which it superseded in Regency work.
Reed moulding (3.04)
Reel and bead turning (2.11)
Refectory table (1.35)
Régence style (see timechart): important transitional style between the main Louis XIV and XV periods, named after but longer than the Orléans Regency (1715–23) for the latter. Cultural life returned from Versailles to Paris and this lighter atmosphere was reflected in more curvaceous furniture, the cabriole leg and the removal of stretchers. Forms included new commodes, the Cressent (1.17) and the *à la Régence*, and the *bergère* armchair (1.05). Ornamentation favoured the lozenge shape, foliate scrolling, espagnolettes (3.06) and ormolu mounts. Slipcovers were an innovation for those not able to afford separate seasonal suites of furniture.

Regency style: painted and gilt sofa c1810

Regency Gothic (see timechart): brief British fashion, inspired by Pugin's father, for Gothic church ornamentation that predated the fuller Gothic revival.
Regency style (see timechart): British style of the early 19th century that drew on Greco-Roman, Egyptian, Chinese and French Empire themes and hence at the time was called English Empire. Named after George IV's regency and reign (1811–30), it extended either side through the pattern books of Sheraton, Hope and George Smith (active 1804–28). 'Grecian' arc-backed chairs (1.09) of *klismos* pattern with scroll arms and sabre legs best exemplify the style's elegance. The sofa table (1.36) was a Regency innovation. Decoration included the acanthus, guilloche, the dolphin and brass inlay.

Renaissance style: Venetian table 16th century

Relief: projecting carving.
Renaissance Revival (see timechart): mid and late 19th century European and American style initiated in Italy, massive and rectangular with a veritable orgy of nationalistic decoration from many sources. Remained particularly popular with the Italian and German public until 1914.
Renaissance style (see timechart): European classical and architecturally-inspired furniture of the 15th to 17th centuries with many phases and national variations. Walnut began to replace oak. New forms included the *cassone* (1.16), mule chest (1.17) and the chest of drawers. Cupboards profilerated into the wardrobe, *armoire* (1.18) and cabinet (1.18).

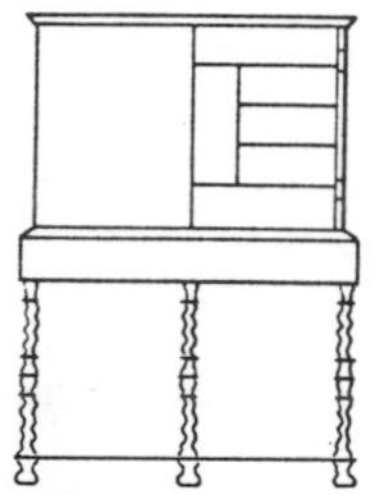
Restoration style: veneered inlaid cabinet on stand, late 17th century

Rent table (1.35)
Reserve: naturally-left area in decoration.
Restauration style (see timechart): Post-Waterloo French Bourbon taste that continued Empire work wholesale except that it removed Napoleonic devices and rejected mahogany for lighter-coloured woods.
Rest bed (1.28)
Restoration style (see timechart): spirited English furniture from the Restoration of Charles II to the Glorious Revolution, the first to adapt continental Baroque. Walnut supplanted oak. Fertile ornamentation bought in spiral turning, scrollwork, deep carving, gesso decoration, and floral marquetry. Caning, lacquering and japanning were all new techniques. Numerous new forms appeared such as the wing chair (1.13), daybed, the slant-front bureau (1.23), in c1670, the *scritoire* writing cabinet (1.24), and small occasional tables.

Riesener: marble-topped commode 1780

Reverse ogee moulding (3.04)
Revolving bookcase (1.30), **chair** (1.11)
Ribband: ribbon ornament.
Ribband back chair (1.11)
Riesener, Jean-Henri [1734–1806]: French Louis XVI cabinetmaker who succeeded Oeben, his teacher, finishing the roll-top *bureau du roi*, and producing his own superlative marquetry-rich work with bronze mounts of his own casting. As King's cabinetmaker 1774–84 he received 900,000 livres' worth of commissions.
Rietveld, Gerrit Thomas [1888–1964]: Dutch De Stijl maker who led the movement in furniture with his Red-Blue armchair design of 1918, a Cubist brightly coloured 'spiritual' but non-functional creation. Influenced Breuer and the Bauhaus yet none of his work was mass-produced.

Rococo style: painted and gilt window seat stool

Rim: raised border edge of a small table.
Rinceau: 18th century French continuous foliage motif.
Ring turning (2.11)
Rising butt hinge (2.12)
Rising stretcher (2.03)
Riven timber: treetrunk split from the perimeter to the centre to create strong planks. Used in Romanesque furniture and since.
Rocking chair (1.11)
Rococo (see timechart): French-originated 18th century asymmetrical furniture

emphasising the S-shaped curve and comfort in reaction to Baroque formality. Improved plush upholstery, Chinoiserie, bright colours, swirling carving, and extravagant marquetry characterised its widely-exported Louis XV zenith of restless frivolity.

Rococo Revival: sofa, Bavaria 1870s

Rococo Revival (see timechart): European and American middle class reenactment of Rococo beginning only 60 years after its eclipse, but this often symmetrical version offered the added comfort of coil-sprung button-backed upholstery, in new French seating forms such as the *indiscret* (1.27), *crapaud* (1.07), *borne* (1.25) and *pouf* (1.11). Dominated 1840s–70s US fashion despite other revivals.

Roentgen, Abraham [1711–93] and **David** [1743–1807]: German Rhineland cabinetmakers with a workshop at Neuwied from 1750. Abraham retired in 1772. David made the business Europe's largest and finest, opening branches in Paris (1774), Vienna, Naples and Prussia (1791). He became Marie Antoinette's cabinetmaker and sold pieces to Catherine the Great; pictorial marquetry being his neoclassical speciality. French Revolutionary troops sacked the Neuwied workshop (1795).

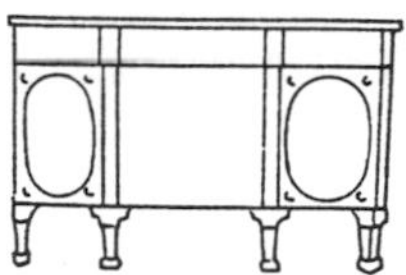

Roentgen: veneered commode with marquetry 1785-95

Rolloret arm (2.02)

Roll top: see Tambour.

Roll top desk (1.23)

Romanesque style (see timechart): early medieval work which rarely survives, an exception is the famous and so-called Dagobert bronze throne, a monumental 8th century Frankish continuation of the Roman X-frame folding chair. Chip carving on brightly-painted riven oak timber predominated in pieces resembling the era's Romanesque architecture.

Romanesque: coffer chest, Brampton church, Northants, England 12th century

Roman style (see timechart): marble, iron, bronze, silver, wooden and wicker furniture of Rome and her empire which re-interpreted Etruscan, Greek, Hellenistic and Egyptian precedents. The commonest chair was the curule (1.07), derived from the Greek *diphros okladias* (1.08). There was the *bisellium* (1.25) double seat (settee); pater familias' *solium* (throne-like seat); an Etruscan tub-like armchair; and the woman's *cathedra*. Among numerous stools the folding *sella* (1.11) was for campaign and administrative use. The *lectus* served as dining couch and bed, being a Greek kline with fulcrum headrest added and in the 1st century AD backs and sides were also fitted. The late imperial *sigma* was a semi-circular couch for six or more diners. The first console tables for sideboard use against a wall appeared as did four-legged tables with stretchers. The cupboard developed with the *armaria* for weapons and the open buffet display board. The movable bronze bath (1.39) became a 19th century standard.

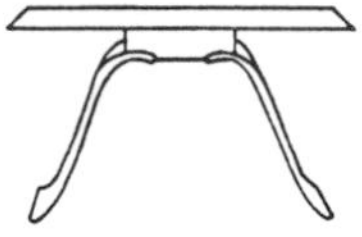

Ruhlmann: ebony macassar table 1930-2

Romayne work: Italian Renaissance decorative roundel or medallion with a person's head in high relief, especially in Iberian and early Tudor work.

Rope chair backs (2.08), **motif** (3.02), **moulding** (3.04)

Rose motif (3.02)

Rosette device (3.02)

Rosewood: multi-species tropical hardwood (eg Bombay and Rio types) so-called due to its scent. Used since the 17th century, particularly for inlay and veneering, being highly polishable and as a solid wood in the 19th century.

Roundabout chair (1.11)

Roundabout/Quaker chair (1.11)

Round billet motif (3.01), **corner joint** (2.16), **escutcheon** (2.13), **moulding** (3.03)

Roundel: small circular device either used singly or in a pattern.

Rowland, David [b1924]: American High-Tech designer since 1955, renowned for his 40-in-4 stacking chair (1964) and Sof-Tech chair (1979), both using plastic and tubular steel.

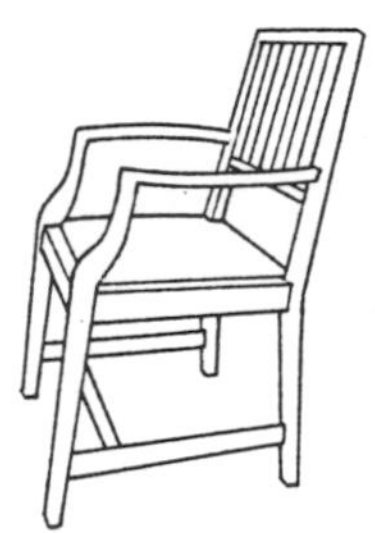

Russell: armchair 1920-30

Rudder table support (2.06)

Rudd/Lady's dressing table (1.35)

Ruhlmann, Jacques-Émile [1879–1933]: foremost French Art Deco designer and maker whose post–1918 workshop produced the style's highest quality work in which the legs look integral with the carcase. From 1930 he shifted into International Modern with pieces for the Palace of the Maharajah of Indore.

Runner: (a) drawer bearer on the bottom or side to aid sliding. (b) rocker stretcher of a rocking chair (2.03). (c) 20th century table surface decorative strip.

Rush seat (2.03)

Russell, Sir Gordon [1892–1980]: British International Style and Utility designer. From a craftsman's family, he began with Cotswold School Arts and Craft Movement work before designing 1930s radio cabinets. He manufactured International Style furniture in London and Worcester, then headed Britain's 1942 wartime Utility programme. After the war he was the Industrial Design Council's first director and opened the Design Centre in 1956.

Saarinen: table by Eero

Rustic chair (1.11)

Saarinen, Eliel [1873–1950] and **Eero** [1910–61]: Finnish-American father and son designers and architects. Eliel designed Art Nouveau furniture before 1900 and emigrated in 1923. He equipped Cranbrook Academy with modern furniture, nursing future designers there starting with Eames. The latter worked with Eero on 1940 designs of storage units and

moulded plywood chairs that led on to Saarinen's fibreglass Womb (1946) and Tulip (1957) chairs (1.13) for Knoll International.
Sabot (3.08): decorative shoe to protect furniture feet since late Louis XIV work.
Sabot foot (2.09)
Sabre leg (2.10)
Sack back Windsor chair (1.15)
Saltire stretcher (2.03)
Sambin, Hugues [c1515–1600]: Burgundian French woodcarver and designer who published a seminal Mannerist pattern book in 1572. Often called the first French cabinetmaker though no work is definitely known to be his.
Sandalwood: Indian aromatic hardwood, easily carved and sometimes a box or small chest material.
Sapele: mahogany-looking West African hardwood used in modern furniture and plywood.
Sash door (2.04): part of a cabinet.
Satin walnut: see Red gum.
Satinwood: yellow hardwoods from the East and West Indies, easily polishable, luxurious and decorative as in late 18th century English work.
Saucer edge top (3.05): table with a raised rim (modern term).
Sausage turning (2.11)
Savonarola chair (1.13): see X-frame chair.
Sawbuck: X-shaped table support, a Gothic and Renaissance feature.
Scagliola: marble compound substitute of Roman times revived in 16th century Italy, widely used for case and table surfaces as well as decoration (highly polishable).
Scaling: fishscale surface décor, common in 18th century Europe.
Scallop: carved shell ornament, notably singly in Spanish decoration and for Rococo floral patterns.
Scandinavian furniture (see timechart): a vanguard post-First World War modern furniture movement marrying fine design to industrial production and materials. Aalto (see entry) and Sweden were its progenitors, followed by Klint (see entry) in Denmark. After 1945 Scandinavian designers, though still often home-based, were working for an appreciative and growing US-led world market.
Scarf joint (2.15)
Schenkschieve cupboard (1.21)
Schragentisch table (1.35)
Schrank cupboard (1.22)
Schuster, Franz [1892–1976]: Austrian unit furniture pioneer from 1927. His work strongly influenced Scandinavian developments.
Sconce (1.38): wall light with a back plate and candle-grease catching pan. Made of metal from the late Middle Ages to c1700 after which looking glasses were preferred as back plates. See Girandole.
Scotia moulding (3.03)
Scratch carving (3.08): a simple form of surface decor using a V-chisel. Normally found on country furniture up to the 18th century.
Screen desk (1.23)
Screens (1.38): a portable structure for shielding people.
Scribe: scoring metal, wood, or other material with a pointer as a guide to cutting.
Scribing (3.05): a joinery method.
Scroll arm (2.02), **back chair** (1.11), **Stay back Windsor chair** (1.15)
Scroll chair back (2.08)
Scroll foot (2.09), **leg** (2.10), **moulding** (3.04), **pediment** (2.14)
Scroll leaf/Scroll work (3.02): decorative device resembling a scroll (from the Ionic column), solid as in armchair arm or a spiral relief as in openwork, see Vitruvian scroll.
Scrolled/Seaweed marquetry: intertwined patterns of tendrils and scrolls, of Italian origin, popular in English William-and-Mary furniture.
Scroll over arm (2.02)
Scroll top leg (2.10)
Sea chest (1.17)
Seat rail (2.02): part of a chair.
Seats (2.03): types of seating construction.
Secretaire/Secretary (1.24): types of desk.
Secretary drawer: fall front drawer providing a surface to write on.
Secret drawer (2.04): concealed part of a cabinet or cupboard, first found from c1650.
Sedan chair (1.11)
Segmental arch form (3.05), **front** (3.05), **stretcher** (2.03), **top** (3.05)
Seiren/Siren device (3.08)
Sella curulis stool (1.11)

Semainier/Chiffonière chest of drawers (1.16)
Sequioa: see Redwood.
Serpentine front: repeated curves.
Serpent nowed and vorant devices (3.08)
Settee (1.28): a seat for two or more persons.
Settle (1.28): a bench with a back and sides.
Sewing table (1.36)
Sezession Movement: Austrian Vienna-based artists who left the Academy in 1897, exhibited Mackintosh's furniture and stimulated Art Nouveau. Josef 'Square' Hoffmann [1870–1956] was the outstanding designer, furnishing his buildings and working for Thonet.
Sgabellor/Board chair (1.11)
Shaft (2.14): part of a pilaster.
Shagreen: dried leather stretched for use as veneering, sharkskin or rayskin being used since the 18th century (especially in Art Deco), white but frequently dyed.
Shaker furniture (1.11, see timechart): austere American rural community work by the Shakers religious sect (founded 1784). They used pine and other local woods for functional, light designs sold cheaply. Most surviving work is post–1860 from five northern states but copies remain popular to this day.
Shaving chair (1.12), **stand** (1.30), **table** (1.36)
Shawl back Windsor chair (1.15)
Shawl chair back (2.08)
Sheaf back chair (1.12), **chair back** (2.08)
Shelf cluster (1.40): mid-Victorian description of display shelves above a mantelpiece.
Shelf joints (2.16)
Shell device (3.08), **foot** (2.09), **front** (3.05), **top** (3.05)
Shellac: an alcohol-soluble natural resin used in French polishing.
Sheraton, Thomas [1751–1806]: English neoclassical designer and trans-Atlantic style setter. His *The Cabinet-Maker and Upholster's Drawing Book* in parts 1791–4 (revised editions 1793, 1802), with 111 engravings, transformed Adam and Hepplewhite into a lighter, more delicate style. *The Cabinet Dictionary* (1803), with 88 engravings, first published Egyptiennerie in Britain and formulated Regency style, as did an unfinished 125-part encyclopedia (1805) that reached the letter C. Ironically, only a glass-fronted bookcase can definitely be attributed to this trained cabinetmaker.

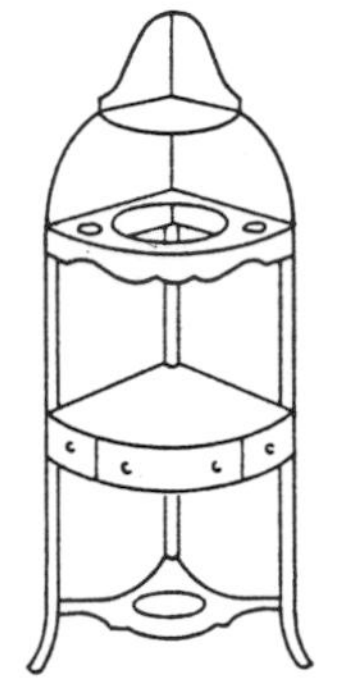
Sheraton: corner basin stand 1791

Sheveret desk (1.23)
Shield back chair (1.12), **chair back** (2.08), **handle** (2.13)
Shovel-Shuttle board: long (up to over 30ft) narrow games table in 17th century England, seldom wider than 3½ft. By the late 18th century it was often relegated to being a servants' dining table.
Siamese sofa (1.28)
Sideboard (1.36)
Side chair (1.12), **panel** (2.04, 2.05), **rail** (2.01, 2.05), **stretcher** (2.02)
Sight size (2.04): visible part of a cabinet glass front.
Silky oak: Australian oak-resembling hardwood, a British 1930s Empire wood.
Sillón de cadera (1.13), **de fraileros chairs** (1.12)
Silver: a solid silver stool survives in the Roman Hildesheim treasure (1st century AD) and silver inlay work was applied in ancient Egypt. Louis XIV briefly set a European royal fashion for silver pieces after Spain had tried to restrict such luxury in the 16th century. Early Georgian mounts and handles were widely silver-plated.
Silver-grey wood: Indian hardwood used in 19th century British marquetry and veneering.
Silvering: use of silver leaf.
Silverwood: Indian hardwood used in 19th century British marquetry.
Silverwood: see Sycamore.
Singerie: vignette of monkeys engaged and dressed as humans, a decorative invention of Bérain (see entry) that proliferated after 1700, frequently with chinoiserie.
Skirting (2.06): see Apron.
Slab-ended stool (1.12)
Slat (2.01): part of a bedstead.
Slat chair back (2.08)
Sledge stretcher (2.03)
Sleeping chair (1.12)
Sleigh bed (1.04)
Slider (2.06): part of a table.
Sliding screens (1.38)
Slip/Loose seat (2.03)
Slipper bath (1.39): 19th century tin bath.
Slipper chair (1.12)
Smoker's bow Windsor chair (1.15)
Sociable double chair (1.28)

Social table (1.36)
Sofas (1.25–1.28): a comfortable upholstered seat for several people.
Sofa bed (1.04), **table** (1.36)
Soffit: architectural terms applied to the underside of a furniture projection.
Softwood: a needle-bearing tree's timber, eg pine spruce, cedar and yew. Generally cheaper than hardwoods. Commonly used in marquetry (easy to stain) and as a secondary wood.
Solid escutcheon (2.13)
Southern/Swamp cypress: sturdy American softwood of varying colour, a feature of 18th century Charleston South Carolinian work.
Spade foot (2.09)
Spanish Colonial style (see timechart): Spanish overseas imperial furniture of the 17th and 18th centuries made chiefly at Mexico City, Lima, Bogota and Quito though Cuba and the Philippines were also major colonies. European in form but often with Indian carving and a more lavish use of silver, mother-of-pearl and other ornament than at home. Mexico continued the *Desornamentado* style while Peru remained faithful to Baroque.
Spanish/Braganza foot (2.09)
Specimen table (1.36)
Sphinx device (3.08)
Spindle (2.02), **back chair** (1.12), **turning** (2.11), **chair back** (2.08), **Windsor chair** (1.15)
Spinet (1.39): small keyboard instrument of 16th century Italian origin. In England they were wing shaped from c1660 and frequently converted to writing desks after 1800.
Spiral leg (2.10)
Splat (2.02): part of a chair back (2.08).
Splay (3.05), **chair back** (2.08), **foot** (2.09): outward-spreading shape.
Splice joint (2.15)
Splint seat (2.03)
Split spindle (3.08), **tail drop handle** (2.13)
Spool turning (2.11)
Spoon back chair (1.12)
Spring upholstery: coiled iron or steel springs in mattresses and cushions. Crude springs were experimented with in Louis XV furniture, but only came into general use after Georg Junigl's spiral metal springs invention (1822) at Vienna which Samuel Pratt patented in London (1828). Consequently, sofa and chair seats became deeper and also deep buttoned to keep the springs in place.
Spruce: strong European and American softwood much used for patented furniture and for the insides of case pieces.
Squab: small armchair cushion since the late 17th century.
Square back chair (1.12), **chair back** (2.08)
Square billet motif (3.01)
Squared handle (2.13), **splice joint** (2.15)
Squirrel-cage: see Birdcage support.
Stag devices (3.08)
Stamped escutcheon (2.13)
Stand table (1.36)
State bed (1.04)
Steamer chair (1.12)
Steel furniture: seldom made until the 20th century, although South German Renaissance examples are known. August Endell produced pieces at Munich during the late 1890s. Tubular steel (hollow rods) has been the real breakthrough since the 1920s.
Stencilling: method of transferring a decorative design through paper or metal. A Gothic furniture skill that is especially significant in early mass-produced US work 1815–60.
Step ladder chair (1.12)
Stepped curve shape (3.05)
Stickley, Gustav [1857–1942]: foremost American Mission furniture (see entry) designer from 1898 of simple settles, sideboards, tables and a variant of the Morris chair (1.10). His brothers left the co-operative in 1901 to market similar rival items. Despite his bankruptcy in 1915, Stickley's ideas influenced Chicago and West Coast designers.
Stick stool (1.12)
Stile (2.02, 2.04): vertical framing member of a piece of furniture, particularly a chair's two rear vertical supports.
Stirrup handle (2.13)
Stools (1.05, 1.07–1.13): a low single seat without arms or back.
Stove grate (1.38): a Chippendale term for a cast iron fire grate.
Straight front (3.05)
Straight moulded leg (2.10)
Strap hinge (2.12)
Strapwork (3.08): carved or painted Mannerist surface décor, first used as carved stucco at

Fontainebleau Palace (1535) to resemble leather bands. Popular in Northern Europe into the 18th century and in American furniture from the 17th century.
Straw chair (1.12)
Straw marquetry: 18th century and early 19th century technique of decorating with coloured straw, notably for small boxes and mirror frames. Many pieces made by French Napoleonic prisoners of war in England.
Stretcher (2.03, 2.06): a strengthening crossbar between legs. A secondary role is that of foot rest. Top makers dispensed with them during the late 18th century.
Stringing: strip of wood, especially holly, boxwood or ebony, inlaid as decoration, narrower than the banding which it often accompanied.
Stripping: removing surface treatments from wooden furniture by chemicals, often caustic soda, and/or sandpaper.
Stirrup handle (2.13)
Stub foot (2.09)
Stump bed (1.04), **bedsteads** (2.01), **leg** (2.10)
Summer bed (1.04)
Sunburst (3.08): symbol of the Macedonian kings and more recently prominent on 18th century case furniture, notably America colonial pieces.
Sunflower device (3.08)
Sunk handle (2.13), **panel and top** (3.05)
Supper Canterbury stand (1.30)
Swag (3.08): surface décor showing a length of ribbon-tied drapery or a garland of flowers and fruits, both derived from real classical temple decoration.
Swan device (3.08), **neck handle** (2.13), **pediments** (2.14)
Sweep front (3.05)
Swell front (3.05), **pediment** (2.14)
Swiss Windsor chair (1.15)
Swords sliding panel (2.06): part of table construction.
Sycamore: hardwood plane wood, dense and light, with maple grain employed for inlay, veneering and panels. See Harewood.
Tabernacle frame (1.40)
Table (1.31–1.37): a horizontal surface on supports.
Table à ecrire (1.37), **à rognon, à l'Italienne, en chiffonnière** (1.36)
Tablecloth: In the Middle Ages luxury fabrics and tapestries mattered more than the pieces under them. Function is both decorative and protective.
Table piano (1.39)
Table rule joint hinge (2.12)
Table top (2.06): part of a table.
Tablet chair back (2.08), **flower motif** (3.01)
Tabouret stool (1.13)
Tailpiece (2.02): see also Windsor chair.
Tallboy/Highboy (US) **chest on chest/chest on stand** (1.17)
Tambour/Roll top (2.04): part of a desk, see Oeben.
Tapered legs (2.10), **shape** (3.05)
Tape seat (2.03)
Tapissier: French upholsterer who belonged to a strict guild before 1791.
Tassel: decorated silk bobble made on a cloth-covered wooden ball, used singly or in line for bed canopies or seat rails. Particularly a Victorian fashion.
Tasselback chair (1.12)
Tatlin, Vladimir [1885–1953]: Russian Constructivist designer who made a curvilinear tubular-steel cantilevered chair in 1927 that Italy mass produced.
Tavern table (1.36)
Tchitola: African hardwood, a walnut look-a-like much favoured as a European veneer.
Tea chest (1.17)
Tea furniture: specialised pieces for the serving of tea became important in 18th century Europe and especially in England. The original tea caddy container became by, c1750, a small rosewood or mahogany chest of circular, octagonal or square shape divided into compartments. The mid-century teapoy (1.37) mounted a caddy on a pedestal table. A normally circular tea kettle stand (1.30) carried the kettle and a spirit lamp. The rimmed tea table (1.37) was first made under Queen Anne to secure cups and serve snacks.
Tea kettle stand (1.30), **table** (1.37)
Teak: heavy Asian hardwood of many varieties (particularly Burmese), decay-resistant.
Telamon: see Atlas (3.06).
Tenon: see Mortise.
Tent bed (1.04)
Term stand (1.30)
Tern foot (2.09)
Tester (2.01): canopy frame and covering of a four-poster bed (1.04).

Tête-a-tête/Vis-a-vis/Siamoise sofa (1.28)
Thonet, Michael [1796–1871]: German designer and mass-manufacturer who patented a revolutionary bentwood (1841) for chair frames thus lightening and curving them. In 1859 he designed the easy-to-assemble bentwood Thonet No 14 chair (1.04), furniture's all-time bestseller that is still being made. Other designs included hat stands, rockers and café chairs. By 1871 Thonet was making 400,000 pieces a year for a worldwide market. Thonet Brothers, having commissioned many 20th century designers, remains in business.
Three back chair back (2.08), **Windsor chair** (1.15)
Throne (1.13): a ceremonial royal or ecclesiastical seat of great symbolic power and often actual magnificence. The oldest known is a stone one from the Cretan Minoan Palace of Knossos (c1800BC). The papal oak and ivory throne of St Peter dates from the 4th century AD.
Through joints (2.17)
Thumb moulding (3.03)
Thumbnail sketch moulding (3.03)
Thuya wood: African softwood whose fine mottling lends it to inlay and veneering.
Tilt top table (1.37)
Toilet glass (1.29)
Toilette en papillon dressing table (1.37)
Tongue: end or edge strip projection for fitting into a groove.
Tongue joints (2.15, 2.16)
Top rail (2.02, 2.04, 2.05), **top** (2.05).
Torchère: see Candlestand.
Tortoise shell: luxurious ornament on Roman furniture and since, especially in Boulle marquetry, where the tortoise shell was really turtle shell.
Torus moulding (3.03)
Toylet table (1.37)
Tracery: Gothic furniture ornamental motif.
Trafalgar/Nelson Windsor chair (1.15)
Transition style (see timechart): two periods of French furniture a century apart. The first coincides with Louis XIV's first years on the throne as Baroque features began to appear. The second, more significant, occupies Louis XV's final years as Rococo furniture began to receive neoclassical ornamentation and more restrained curves.
Treble arched pediment (2.14)
Tree devices (3.08)
Trefoil: single or repeated three-lobed leaf motif in Gothic tracery.
Trestle: movable beams with legs used as furniture supports since the Middle Ages.
Trestle table (1.37)
Tricoteuse table (1.37)
Tric trac table (1.37)
Triddarn cupboard (1.22): peculiar to North Wales and the Lake District.
Tripod light (1.38): a triple candelabrum.
Tripod screen (1.38), **table** (1.37)
Triquetra device (3.08)
Trophy: classical motif of arms and armour (and less frequently symbols of other arts such as music) especially revived on Louis XIV and Empire martial pieces.
Troumadarn table (1.37)
Truckle/Trundle bed (1.04)
Trumeau (1.40): Louis XV-XVI mirror with painting above.
Trumpet leg (2.10), **turning** (2.11)
Trunk (1.17)
Truss (2.06): part of a table.
Tub bath (1.39), **chair** (1.09)
Tudor style (see timechart): English predominantly 16th century furniture in a Renaissance, increasingly Mannerist-influenced provincial style. It developed the draw-leaf table (1.33) by 1550; the decorative Nonsuch chest (1.17); and the Farthingale chair (1.08) (the latter two being 19th century names). Holly and ebony were new woods. The reign of Elizabeth I is sometimes separated from the four earlier Tudors, but in fact the ornate Italianate trend only became more pronounced.
Tufting: upholstery tied down by a sewn button.
Tulip/Yellow poplar/American whitewood: pale green-streaked American East Coast hardwood used for drawers, interiors and Windsor seats.
Tulip chair (1.13): see Saarienen.
Tulipwood/Pinkwood (US): Brazilian hardwood very similar to rosewood, much used in Louis XV marquetry despite its awkward working.
Tupelo: gumwood hardwood of South Eastern USA for framing and plywood. Often stained to look like mahogany or walnut for cheaper pieces.
Turkey wood: English 17th century upholstery embroidery inspired by oriental carpets.

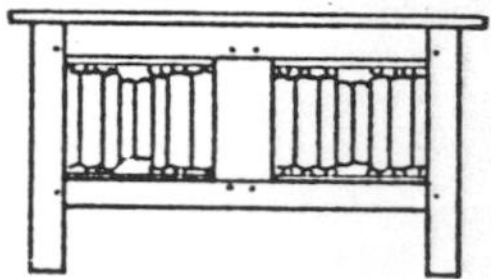
Tudor style: chest c1500

Utility furniture: dressing table and stool 1946

Van de Velde: armchair 1894-5

Vile and Cobb: mahogany library desk by Vile c1745

Turned/'Thrown' chair (1.13)
Turned and fluted turnery (2.11)
Turnery (2.11): wood carved on a lathe.
Turnip foot (2.09)
Turtle back: elliptical or round boss decoration on Jacobean case pieces.
Tuscan bed (1.04)
Tuscan order: a simple and derived order of Roman classical architecture.
Twist turning (2.11)
Uberauschrank (1.22)
Umbrella stand (1.30)
Unit furniture: modular work since innovatory German designs of the 1920s. The aims are standard shapes, multi-purpose versatility and economy of space.
Upholstered back (2.02), **seat** (2.03)
Upholstery: textile stretching across, covering, padding and stuffing of seats and furniture surrounds for greater comfort and decoration. In late 16th century France cushion and padding were combined and tacked to the frame. Horsehair was for long the commonest stuffing. Modern synthetic materials have streamlined the traditional upholstered look. See Spring upholstery.
Urn: Renaissance-revived classical vase-like ornament. Used as a finial and at stretcher intersections, most especially on neoclassical work.
Utility furniture (see style timechart): Britain's Second World War official programme to ration furniture production into a few simple rectlinear designs. Its inexpensive quality proved popular and left a functional design legacy.
Vaisselier cupboard (1.22)
Valance (2.01): horizontal length of drapery on a bed canopy or curtains. See Apron and Lambrequin.
Van de Velde, Henri [1863–1957]: Belgian Art Nouveau architect, designer, and propagandist of modernism. He made geometric, abstract furniture for his 1894–5 home and for the Paris gallery L'Art Nouveau. In Germany and Switzerland 1899–1924 he shifted towards Bauhaus functionalism.
Vargueño desk (1.23)
Varnish: clear liquid resin coating for finishing and beautifying wood. Used in ancient Egypt and revived in 17th century Europe with oil-based types. Glossier alcohol-based varieties came from the Far East c1670. Modern varnish is a 19th century-invented paint made of cellulose.
Vase turnings (2.11)
Veneer: very thin cut sheets of wood or other material applied to other surfaces as decoration and protection. A skill dating back to antiquity and revived by intarsia (see entry). In wide use from the mid–17th century starting from the Low Countries (ebony, ivory and turtle shell).
Verdigris: lightish green paint on wood to represent the texture of ancient bronze. See Antique vert.
Vernis Martin: French japanning technique perfected by the four Martin brothers c1730–70. The main constituent was copal varnish which gave a rich and shiny surface.
Vertical grain panel (3.05)
Vienna chair (1.13)
Vignette motif (3.02)
Vile and Cobb (active c1750–78): famous London makers of expensive Rococo mahogany work, especially case pieces for George III.
Violet wood: see Kingwood.
Virola: very light South American hardwood confined to interior work and mainly in the Americas.
Vis-à-vis/Tête-à-tête/Siamoise sofa (1.28)
Vitrine table (1.37)
Vitruvian scroll (running dog): neoclassical decorative motif of architectural origin used on case cornices and table top frieze rails, notably in Palladian style work.
Vol device (3.08)
Volute (2.14)
Voyeuse chair (1.13)
Vredeman de Vries, Hans [c1527–post 1604] and **Paul** [1567–post 1630]: Dutch designers who published much-imitated Mannerist pattern books in 1560–88 and 1630 respectively. Their carving and ornamentation designs prevailed across Northern Europe late in the 17th century. Hans was also an Auricular style creator.
Wagon seat sofa (1.28)
Wainscot chair (1.13)
Walnut: richly marked European and North American hardwood and a major furniture material since antiquity. Easy to cut, carve and polish. Revived in the Renaissance, it dominated English work c1660-c1730 until mahogany gained first place.

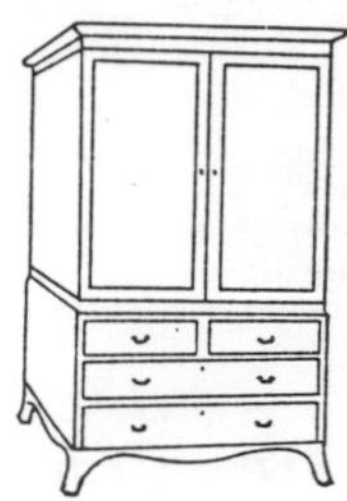

Wardrobe: design from Hepplewhite's *Guide* (3rd ed, 1794)

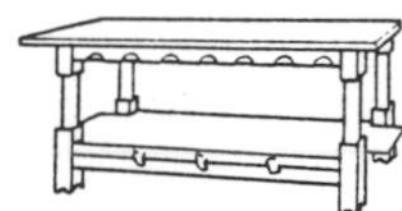

Webb: table c1870

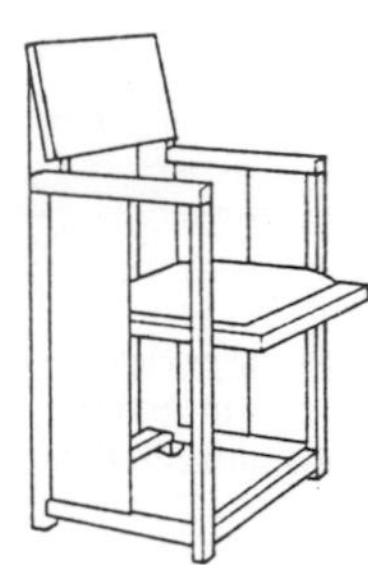

Wright: armchair 1904

Wardrobe: case furniture for storing clothing. Evolved from the medieval press in the 16th and 17th centuries. The modern form and name emerged in the 18th century with hanger rail and mirror. Door hinge (2.12).
Wash hand stand (1.30)
Waterbed (1.04)
Waterleaf (3.02): popular decorative motifs on neoclassical furniture.
Wave motif (3.01)
Waving slat chair back (2.08)
Webb, Philip Speakman [1831–1915]: late Victorian British architect and designer of the c1865 Morris chair (1.10) as William Morris' firm's chief designer in the Arts and Crafts Movement. From 1875 he concentrated on pieces integrated with his buildings.
Wegner, Hans [b1914]: Danish Modern designer of handmade but functional wooden work since 1940 such as his Peacock chair (1947), which triumphantly marries traditional cabinetmaking skills to streamlined design.
Welsh dresser cupboard (1.22)
Wenge: streaked West African hardwood of growing popularity for European framing and veneering.
West Indian satinwood: creamy yellow Caribbean hardwood whose beauty appealed to neoclassical makers either side of the Atlantic, but it is now rare and replaced by the Ceylon variety.
What not/Etagère stand (1.30)
Wheel back Windsor chair (1.15)
Wheatsheaf chair back (2.08)
Wheatshuck device (3.08)
Wheel chair (1.13), **chair back** (2.08)
Whiplash curve device (3.08): Art Nouveau ornament.
Whitebeam: European hardwood not unlike pearwood and used as veneering.
Whorl device (3.08)
Wicker chair (1.13)
Wicker furniture: woven pieces, a craft derived from ancient basket making. Rattan was the most common 19th century material ousting willow shoots. The basket chair (1.05) is the most typical form and was made in the Roman Empire. Wicker pieces are light and handy so being suitable for outdoor and summer use.
Wig stand (1.30)
William and Mary style (see timechart): end 17th century English Baroque furniture much influenced by the Dutch and Huguenot designers in the royal couple's household. Made of walnut with Dutch marquetry and oyster veneer. New forms were the 1690s bureau, bookcase (1.24), the card table (1.32) and the tea table (1.37). Carved scroll supports and the baluster were popular details.
Windsor chairs (1.14, 1.15), **settee** (1.28): traditional form, wooden seat and stick back.
Wine cooler (1.30): not all are cellarets (see entry). The heyday for tub-like wine-coolers with removable tops was c1755–1830. These Georgian pieces were often brass bound and sometimes urn (Adam) or sarcophogus (Regency) shaped.
Wine table and stand (1.37)
Wing/Grandfather chair (1.13)
Wing clothes press cupboard (1.22), **wardrobe** (1.22)
Work stand (1.30)
Wreath device (3.08)
Wright, Frank Lloyd [1867–1959]: American architect and designer who started furniture making in 1895 to exaggerated linear designs. His Larkin Administration Building (Buffalo, New York, till 1950) contained the world's first purpose-built steel office furniture. The same year saw his geometric cube wooden chair, and Japonisme became a powerful influence from 1905. After 1915 sculptural and architectural qualities prevailed at the expense of comfort.
Writing arm (2.02), **Windsor chair** (1.15)
Writing box (1.17), **cabinet** (1.22), **chair** (1.13), **table** (1.37)
Wycombe style Windsor chair (1.15)
Wyvern device (3.08)
X-frame chair (1.13), **chair back** (2.08), **stretcher** (2.03)
Yellow wood: softwood from Central America, exported as fustic for 18th century British inlay details.
Yew: hard reddish European softwood used in furniture since antiquity. Polishable and workable, it has been the standard bentwood for Windsor chairs as well as veneer/inlay wood since the 17th century.
Yorkshire chair (1.13)
Zanzibar chair (1.13)
Zebrawood: African hardwood employed as a colourful marquetry.
Zig zag motif (3.01)

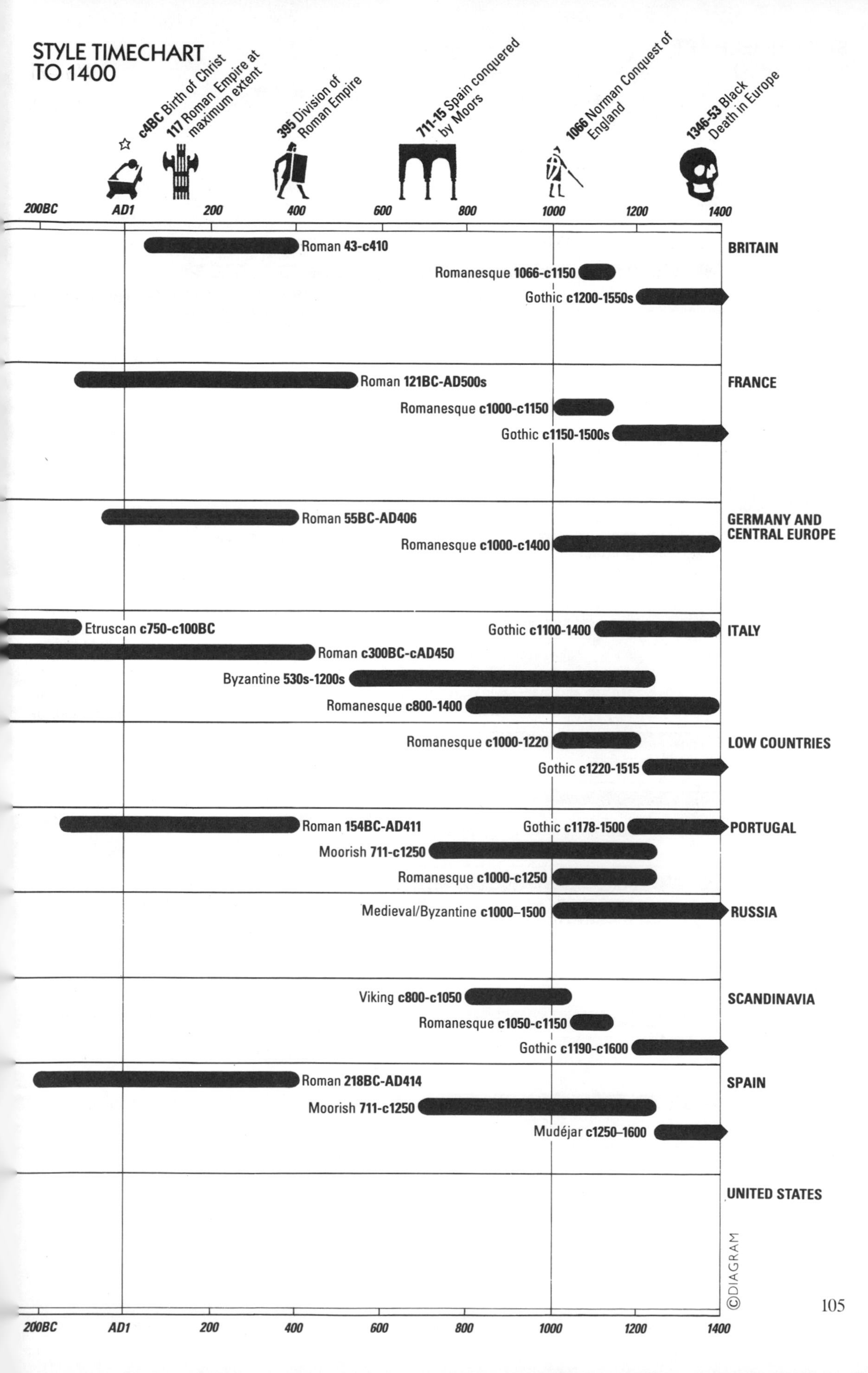
STYLE TIMECHART TO 1400
c4BC Birth of Christ
117 Roman Empire at maximum extent
395 Division of Roman Empire
711-15 Spain conquered by Moors
1066 Norman Conquest of England
1346-53 Black Death in Europe
200BC
AD1
200
400
600
800
1000
1200
1400
BRITAIN
Roman 43-c410
Romanesque 1066-c1150
Gothic c1200-1550s
FRANCE
Roman 121BC-AD500s
Romanesque c1000-c1150
Gothic c1150-1500s
GERMANY AND CENTRAL EUROPE
Roman 55BC-AD406
Romanesque c1000-c1400
ITALY
Etruscan c750-c100BC
Gothic c1100-1400
Roman c300BC-cAD450
Byzantine 530s-1200s
Romanesque c800-1400
LOW COUNTRIES
Romanesque c1000-1220
Gothic c1220-1515
PORTUGAL
Roman 154BC-AD411
Gothic c1178-1500
Moorish 711-c1250
Romanesque c1000-c1250
RUSSIA
Medieval/Byzantine c1000–1500
SCANDINAVIA
Viking c800-c1050
Romanesque c1050-c1150
Gothic c1190-c1600
SPAIN
Roman 218BC-AD414
Moorish 711-c1250
Mudéjar c1250–1600
UNITED STATES
©DIAGRAM
200BC
AD1
200
400
600
800
1000
1200
1400

STYLE TIMECHART 1400–1800

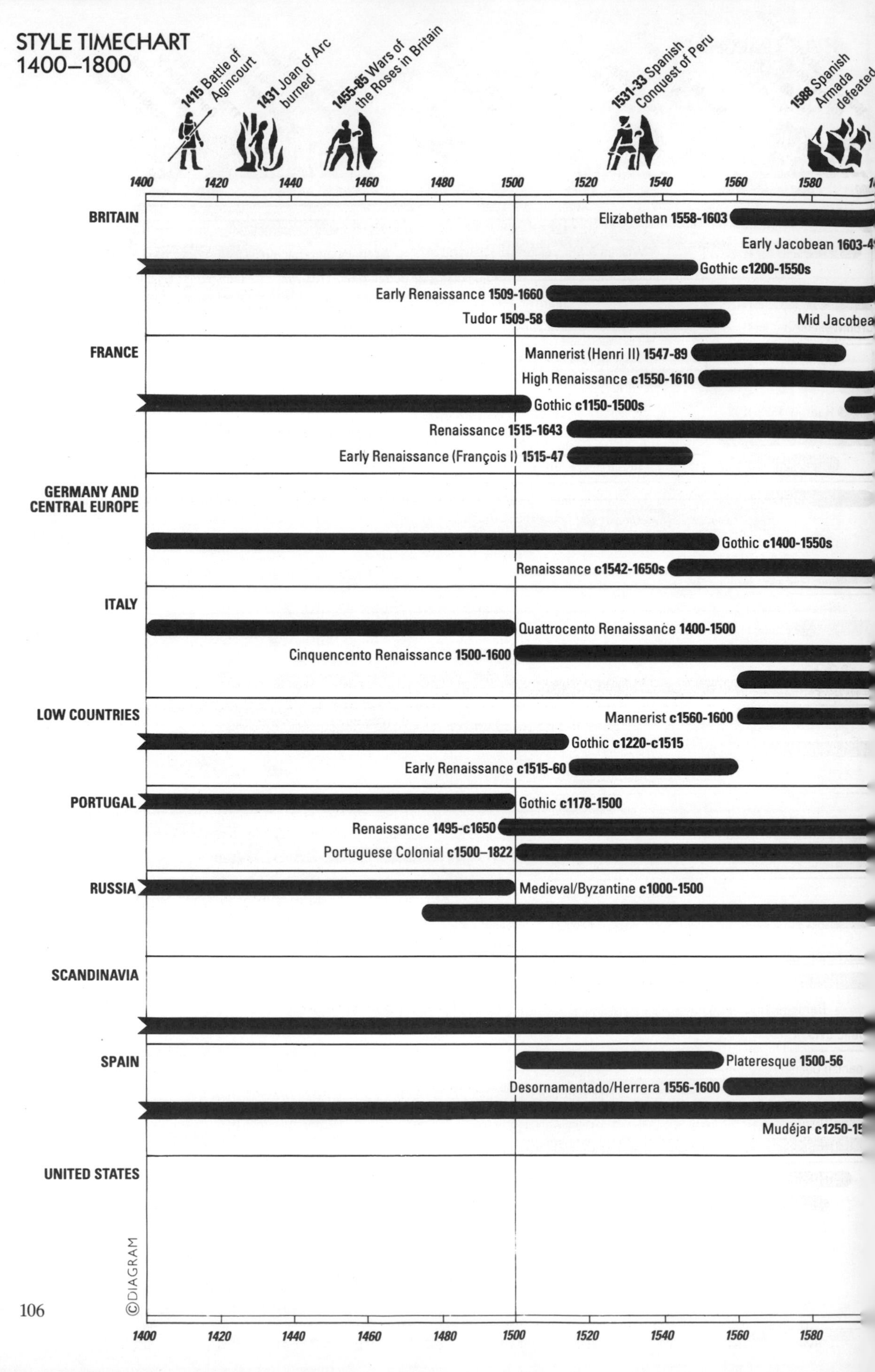
1415 Battle of Agincourt
1431 Joan of Arc burned
1455-85 Wars of the Roses in Britain
1531-33 Spanish Conquest of Peru
1588 Spanish Armada defeated
1400
1420
1440
1460
1480
1500
1520
1540
1560
1580
BRITAIN
Elizabethan 1558-1603
Early Jacobean 1603-4
Gothic c1200-1550s
Early Renaissance 1509-1660
Tudor 1509-58
Mid Jacobea
FRANCE
Mannerist (Henri II) 1547-89
High Renaissance c1550-1610
Gothic c1150-1500s
Renaissance 1515-1643
Early Renaissance (François I) 1515-47
GERMANY AND CENTRAL EUROPE
Gothic c1400-1550s
Renaissance c1542-1650s
ITALY
Quattrocento Renaissance 1400-1500
Cinquencento Renaissance 1500-1600
LOW COUNTRIES
Mannerist c1560-1600
Gothic c1220-c1515
Early Renaissance c1515-60
PORTUGAL
Gothic c1178-1500
Renaissance 1495-c1650
Portuguese Colonial c1500–1822
RUSSIA
Medieval/Byzantine c1000-1500
SCANDINAVIA
SPAIN
Plateresque 1500-56
Desornamentado/Herrera 1556-1600
Mudéjar c1250-15
UNITED STATES
1400
1420
1440
1460
1480
1500
1520
1540
1560
1580

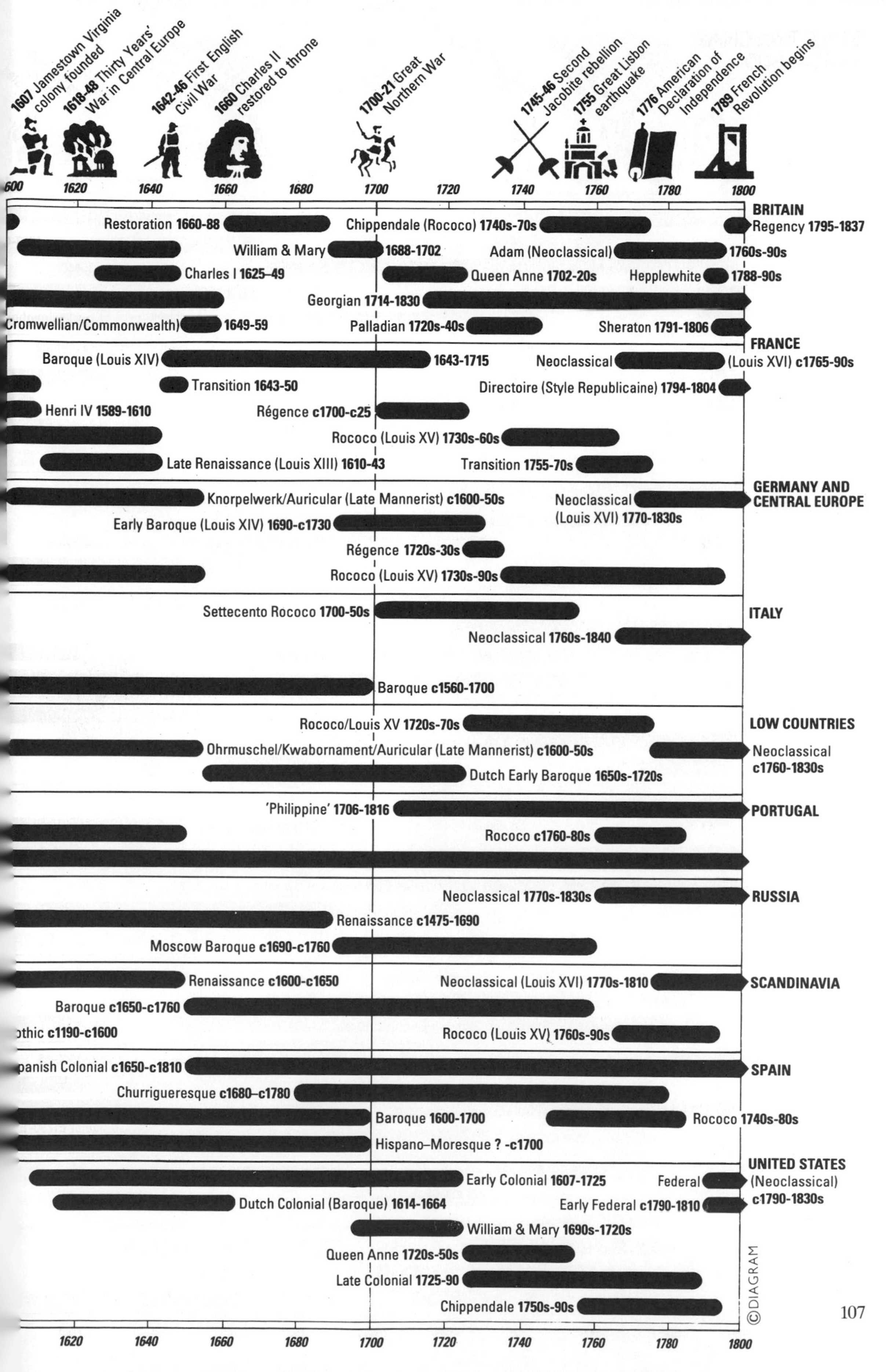

1607 Jamestown Virginia colony founded
1618-48 Thirty Years' War in Central Europe
1642-46 First English Civil War
1660 Charles II restored to throne
1700-21 Great Northern War
1745-46 Second Jacobite rebellion
1755 Great Lisbon earthquake
1776 American Declaration of Independence
1789 French Revolution begins
1600
1620
1640
1660
1680
1700
1720
1740
1760
1780
1800
BRITAIN
Restoration 1660-88
Chippendale (Rococo) 1740s-70s
Regency 1795-1837
William & Mary 1688-1702
Adam (Neoclassical) 1760s-90s
Charles I 1625-49
Queen Anne 1702-20s
Hepplewhite 1788-90s
Georgian 1714-1830
Cromwellian/Commonwealth) 1649-59
Palladian 1720s-40s
Sheraton 1791-1806
FRANCE
Baroque (Louis XIV) 1643-1715
Neoclassical (Louis XVI) c1765-90s
Transition 1643-50
Directoire (Style Republicaine) 1794-1804
Henri IV 1589-1610
Régence c1700-c25
Rococo (Louis XV) 1730s-60s
Late Renaissance (Louis XIII) 1610-43
Transition 1755-70s
GERMANY AND CENTRAL EUROPE
Knorpelwerk/Auricular (Late Mannerist) c1600-50s
Neoclassical (Louis XVI) 1770-1830s
Early Baroque (Louis XIV) 1690-c1730
Régence 1720s-30s
Rococo (Louis XV) 1730s-90s
ITALY
Settecento Rococo 1700-50s
Neoclassical 1760s-1840
Baroque c1560-1700
LOW COUNTRIES
Rococo/Louis XV 1720s-70s
Ohrmuschel/Kwabornament/Auricular (Late Mannerist) c1600-50s
Neoclassical c1760-1830s
Dutch Early Baroque 1650s-1720s
PORTUGAL
'Philippine' 1706-1816
Rococo c1760-80s
RUSSIA
Neoclassical 1770s-1830s
Renaissance c1475-1690
Moscow Baroque c1690-c1760
SCANDINAVIA
Renaissance c1600-c1650
Neoclassical (Louis XVI) 1770s-1810
Baroque c1650-c1760
othic c1190-c1600
Rococo (Louis XV) 1760s-90s
SPAIN
panish Colonial c1650-c1810
Churrigueresque c1680–c1780
Baroque 1600-1700
Rococo 1740s-80s
Hispano–Moresque ? -c1700
UNITED STATES
Early Colonial 1607-1725
Federal (Neoclassical) c1790-1830s
Dutch Colonial (Baroque) 1614-1664
Early Federal c1790-1810
William & Mary 1690s-1720s
Queen Anne 1720s-50s
Late Colonial 1725-90
Chippendale 1750s-90s
©DIAGRAM
1620
1640
1660
1680
1700
1720
1740
1760
1780
1800

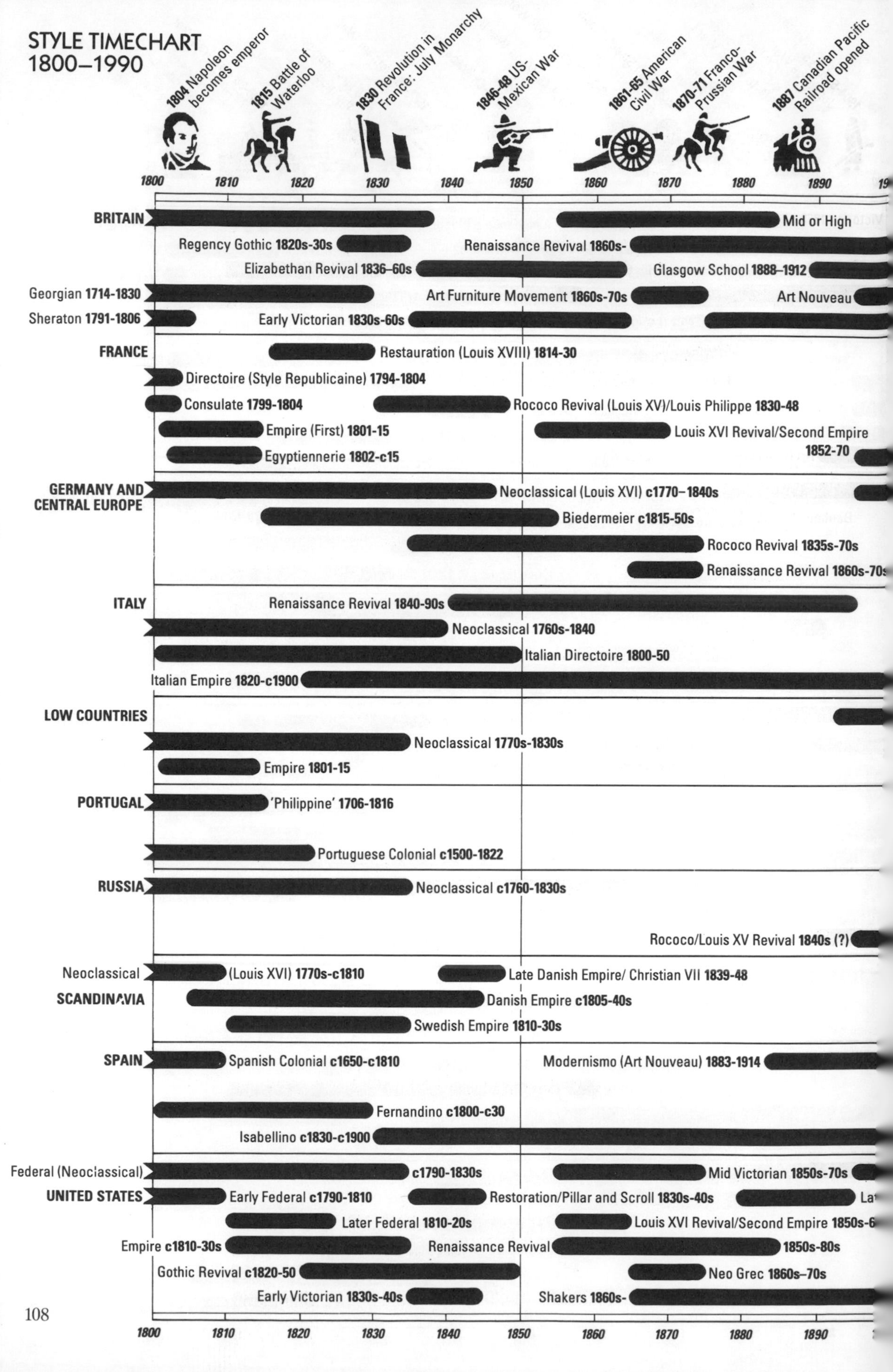
STYLE TIMECHART
1800–1990
1804 Napoleon becomes emperor
1815 Battle of Waterloo
1830 Revolution in France: July Monarchy
1846-48 US-Mexican War
1861-65 American Civil War
1870-71 Franco-Prussian War
1887 Canadian Pacific Railroad opened
1800
1810
1820
1830
1840
1850
1860
1870
1880
1890
BRITAIN
Mid or High
Regency Gothic 1820s-30s
Renaissance Revival 1860s-
Elizabethan Revival 1836–60s
Glasgow School 1888–1912
Georgian 1714-1830
Art Furniture Movement 1860s-70s
Art Nouveau
Sheraton 1791-1806
Early Victorian 1830s-60s
FRANCE
Restauration (Louis XVIII) 1814-30
Directoire (Style Republicaine) 1794-1804
Consulate 1799-1804
Rococo Revival (Louis XV)/Louis Philippe 1830-48
Empire (First) 1801-15
Louis XVI Revival/Second Empire
1852-70
Egyptiennerie 1802-c15
GERMANY AND CENTRAL EUROPE
Neoclassical (Louis XVI) c1770–1840s
Biedermeier c1815-50s
Rococo Revival 1835s-70s
Renaissance Revival 1860s-70s
ITALY
Renaissance Revival 1840-90s
Neoclassical 1760s-1840
Italian Directoire 1800-50
Italian Empire 1820-c1900
LOW COUNTRIES
Neoclassical 1770s-1830s
Empire 1801-15
PORTUGAL
'Philippine' 1706-1816
Portuguese Colonial c1500-1822
RUSSIA
Neoclassical c1760-1830s
Rococo/Louis XV Revival 1840s (?)
Neoclassical
(Louis XVI) 1770s-c1810
Late Danish Empire/ Christian VII 1839-48
SCANDINAVIA
Danish Empire c1805-40s
Swedish Empire 1810-30s
SPAIN
Spanish Colonial c1650-c1810
Modernismo (Art Nouveau) 1883-1914
Fernandino c1800-c30
Isabellino c1830-c1900
Federal (Neoclassical)
c1790-1830s
Mid Victorian 1850s-70s
UNITED STATES
Early Federal c1790-1810
Restoration/Pillar and Scroll 1830s-40s
Later Federal 1810-20s
Louis XVI Revival/Second Empire 1850s-6
Empire c1810-30s
Renaissance Revival
1850s-80s
Gothic Revival c1820-50
Neo Grec 1860s–70s
Early Victorian 1830s-40s
Shakers 1860s-
1800
1810
1820
1830
1840
1850
1860
1870
1880
1890

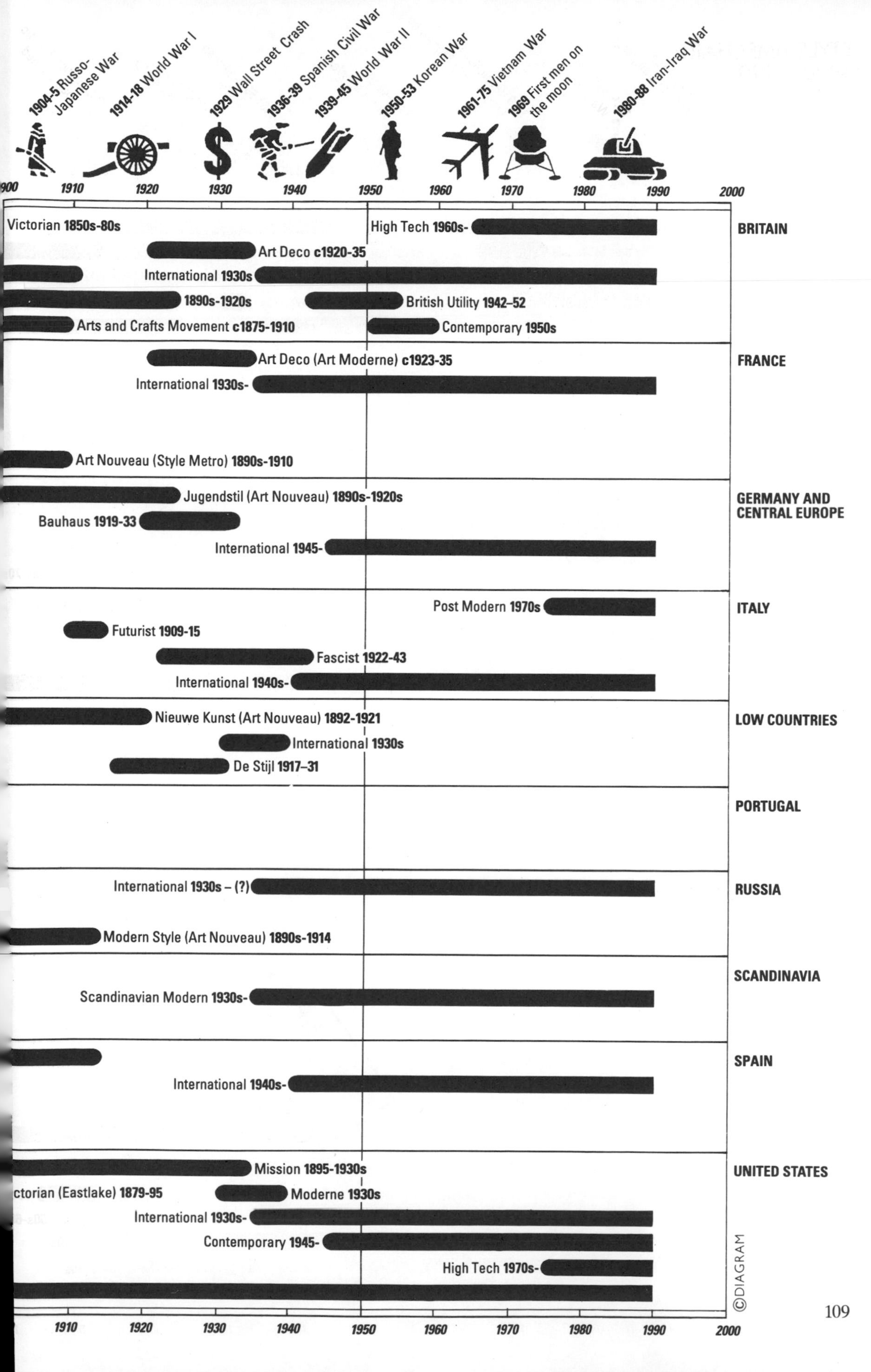

1904-5 Russo-Japanese War
1914-18 World War I
1929 Wall Street Crash
1936-39 Spanish Civil War
1939-45 World War II
1950-53 Korean War
1961-75 Vietnam War
1969 First men on the moon
1980-88 Iran-Iraq War
1900 1910 1920 1930 1940 1950 1960 1970 1980 1990 2000
BRITAIN
Victorian 1850s-80s
High Tech 1960s-
Art Deco c1920-35
International 1930s
1890s-1920s
British Utility 1942–52
Arts and Crafts Movement c1875-1910
Contemporary 1950s
FRANCE
Art Deco (Art Moderne) c1923-35
International 1930s-
Art Nouveau (Style Metro) 1890s-1910
GERMANY AND CENTRAL EUROPE
Jugendstil (Art Nouveau) 1890s-1920s
Bauhaus 1919-33
International 1945-
ITALY
Post Modern 1970s
Futurist 1909-15
Fascist 1922-43
International 1940s-
LOW COUNTRIES
Nieuwe Kunst (Art Nouveau) 1892-1921
International 1930s
De Stijl 1917–31
PORTUGAL
RUSSIA
International 1930s – (?)
Modern Style (Art Nouveau) 1890s-1914
SCANDINAVIA
Scandinavian Modern 1930s-
SPAIN
International 1940s-
UNITED STATES
Mission 1895-1930s
ctorian (Eastlake) 1879-95
Moderne 1930s
International 1930s-
Contemporary 1945-
High Tech 1970s-
1910 1920 1930 1940 1950 1960 1970 1980 1990 2000